The Cook's Dictionary

Published by
Nickel Press

acorn squash

A green squash shaped somewhat like an acorn with deep ridges running from top to bottom, ranging in size from about four to six inches in diameter.

Our favorite (and easiest) squash recipe

Split an acorn squash in half from top to bottom, then scrape out the seeds and fiber. Cut a thin strip from the shell to allow the squash to lay cut side up without toppling. Place halves in a baking pan and surround with about ½ inch of water. Spread the hollows with a little butter or margarine and sprinkle with cinnamon. Pour in a little maple or fruit syrup, if desired. Bake at 350° for about forty minutes, or until tender. Serve the halves or cut into quarters if the squash is very large.

aioli sauce

A basic garlic sauce that, like most other sauces, has a host of variations. Aioli sauce is commonly served over hot or cold seafood, cold meat, salad, or cooked vegetables.

If you have ever experienced the agony of homemade mayonnaise that would not thicken or are concerned about foods that contain raw eggs, you will understand why we have not included a recipe here. Suffice it to say that a credible substitute can be made by blending  one-half cup of commercial mayonnaise with two to three cloves of minced garlic, one-half teaspoon lemon juice and, if you like, one-quarter teaspoon dried mustard.

agar or agar-agar

A gelatin obtained from seaweed, used in aspics and jelled desserts; it is not easily broken down by heat or acidic fruit.

aglio olio

Spaghetti with oil and garlic, made by soaking about six cloves of finely chopped garlic in one-half to three-quarters of a cup of warm olive oil for a few minutes, then tossing with one to two cups of cooked spaghetti and a dash of freshly ground pepper. Serve garnished with chopped fresh parsley, basil, and thyme.

à la carte

French—literally, *on the menu.* A term designating that items on a menu are priced individually.

à la king

French—*in the style of the king.* Designating a dish in which the main ingredients are diced and served in a cream sauce, often containing pimientos, mushrooms, etc.

à la mode

French—*fashionable.* In the prevailing style, or of a certain style, such as pie or other dessert served with ice cream.

al burro

Certainly among the simplest of Italian dishes—*al burro* merely describes spaghetti that has been tossed with butter, a delightful accompaniment to a spicy meat or vegetable entree.

alcohol

A colorless, volatile liquid that is the intoxicating element in fermented or distilled beverages. Alcohol is included here to make a couple of points:

- Those who normally shun alcoholic beverages may nevertheless want to consider their use to flavor certain dishes. Alcohol in a beverage evaporates in the course of heating just as it does in flavorings such as vanilla or lemon extract that may contain as much as 80% alcohol.
- Don't hesitate to experiment when cooking with beer, wine or a distilled beverage. In the course of cooking, some flavors are intensified, while others may change or become overshadowed by another seasoning.

Tip: Avoid *cooking wine* as it is extremely salty and often lacking in flavor. Better to use an inexpensive drinking wine.

al dente

Italian—*to the tooth.* Descriptive of cooked pasta that remains firm so that it offers a slight resistance when bitten.

ale

A popular British **beer** produced by top-fermentation, character-ized by a distinctive yeasty taste and aroma.

Contrary to popular notion, an ale is not necessarily stronger than any other type of beer as the alcohol content can be con-trolled in the brewing process.

allspice

A reddish-brown berry whose name reflects the fact that it releases a flavor reminiscent of a combination of cinnamon, nutmeg and clove. Available as a whole dried berry or finely ground, allspice is used to flavor marinades, spice cakes, and pickling solutions.

almond

A mild-flavored nut, relatively high in protein and oil. Almonds are commonly available roasted or blanched with the skins re-moved, but are more likely to be fresh, flavorful, and less expen-sive if bought in the shell. Use almonds whole, sliced, or chopped and blended with butter to flavor fish or vegetables; ground up to flavor desserts; or eaten whole with fruit and cheese.

❋ When fresh, use them to make almond butter—they are so rich in oil that there is no need to add any—just salt to taste.

Tip: To blanch almonds, simply pour boiling water over them, drain quickly, and rinse in cold water to prevent destruction of the natural oils. Drain them again and rub the skins off.

aluminum see cookware

amaretto

A mild, almond-flavored liqueur often served with coffee or used to flavor desserts.

ambrosia

❋ In Greek and Roman mythology, the food of the gods. Com-monly used to describe anything that is especially delicious or fragrant.

❋ A dessert containing, among other things, oranges and flaked coconut.

anchovy

These salty little fishes that come bathed in oil have a common bond with foods such as buttermilk and liver—they are either loved or hated; few people are casual about their attitude toward them. And while we believe it is foolish to attempt to convert anyone, we do feel that even those who have an aversion should be informed that these little rascals can be used to add a flavor that is neither salty nor fishy:

⁕ A modest amount of *anchovy butter*, a mixture of mashed anchovies and butter or margarine, can be melted on a steak or added to an otherwise bland cooked vegetable to impart a delightful flavor.

⁕ In northern Italy they create a wonderful dip or **fondue** called *bagna cauda* by cooking six to eight mashed anchovy fillets and four to six mashed or minced cloves of garlic in one-half cup of butter and one-half cup of olive oil over low heat for five or ten minutes. Stir often to keep the garlic from scorching, place on a hot-plate or in a fondue dish to keep warm, and serve as a dipping sauce with a variety of chilled vegetables such as cherry tomatoes, carrot sticks, celery sticks, lettuce leaves, and pepper strips. It's a truly unique flavor that makes an interesting appetizer or featured course for a summer brunch.

angel-hair pasta

A very thin **spaghetti**.

Most of us are accustomed to dried pasta that requires longer cooking than the fresh variety. Although cooking times vary depending on how long the package has been on the shelf, be aware that even dried angel-hair may cook almost as quickly as a fresh pasta, requiring only a couple of minutes. See also, **pasta**.

Tip: Not only do the delicate strands of angel-hair pasta require less cooking, they require less flavoring and thus are delicious as a side dish tossed only in butter (*al burro*), a blend of warm olive oil and minced garlic (*aglio olio*), or a light cream sauce.

anise
A variety of herb with a licorice-like taste whose seeds, appropriately called *aniseed* are used mainly to flavor cakes, cookies, breads, pickles, etc.

anisette
A clear liqueur flavored with anise, served with coffee or used as a flavoring.

antipasto
Italian—before food. An assortment of fresh or marinated vegetables, cured fish or meat, cheeses and olives served as an appetizer.

apéritif
Wine that has been flavored with herbs, usually served before a meal. Commonly, any alcoholic beverage taken before a meal.

appetizer
A small portion of food or drink served at the beginning of a meal.

❋ An appetizer should be full-flavored to stimulate the palate for the food that is to come, but served in modest portions so as not to quell one's hunger.

Tip: For a special meal, begin with an appetizer treat that is too rich or expensive to serve as a main course.

Another Tip: For an elegant light brunch or supper, serve a variety of appetizers in succession and eliminate the main course.

apple
A fruit common to North America that finds its way into a variety of foods: as a relish, a flavor additive to both meat and vegetable dishes, and the main ingredient of a host of desserts.

apple butter
Not a butter at all, but a delightful spread or garnish nevertheless, made by cooking apple chunks in water or cider until they are soft; passing the resulting pulp through a strainer; combining it with sugar, cinnamon, cloves and allspice to taste; then cooking again slowly while stir-

ring until it has thickened. Serve as a spread for bread, as a relish with a savory meat dish, or with fruit and cheese.

apple cider

The pure juice of the apple. Those familiar with the taste of fresh apple cider will eschew those insipid frozen or preservative-laden excuses and opt for fresh only. In cooler climes, a jug of cider keeps well on the back porch out of the sun—and if it starts to turn and gets a little tang to it, so much the better. But be wary, for once started, it turns quickly.

Tip: When fresh cider turns and becomes acidic: if there is no mold you may want to taste to see if you have become the fortunate beneficiary of a full-bodied apple vinegar.

apple corer

A cylindrical or half-round blade for removing the core from an apple or other fruit. There is also a device with blades emanating like the spokes of a wheel from a small cylinder, designed to cut the fruit into sections as it cores.

applejack

A brandy distilled in the United States from fermented apple cider. Like its French counterpart *Calvados*, applejack is a *fruit brandy*, that is to say it is distilled from the fruit, not flavored with it (in which case it would have to be labeled *apple-flavored brandy*).

applesauce

A relish or dessert made from cooked apples in much the same fashion as **apple butter**, except that it is usually lightly spiced with cinnamon or nutmeg and cooked only long enough to soften and blend the flavors.

apricot

A small fruit related to the plum, the apricot's distinctive flavor is used in much the same way as the apple's: to grace the table with relishes, add a fruity flavor to savory dishes, in the distillation of spirits, and as the basis for many desserts.

Drying apricots, as with most foods, intensifies the flavor. Dried apricots may be reconstituted by simmering for about thirty minutes in water, then adding sugar to taste and continuing to cook until the sugar has dissolved.

arrowroot

A thickener similar to cornstarch, used for the most delicate of sauces. Unlike flour or cornstarch, arrowroot has a neutral flavor and does not have to be cooked to rid it of a raw taste. It also thickens at a lower temperature, making it ideal for sauces that should not boil. Sauces made with arrowroot must be served immediately after being prepared, however, as they do not hold well and cannot be reheated.

Tip: To avoid lumping, mix with a small amount of water before adding to a hot liquid, allowing a scant tablespoon of arrowroot for each cup of liquid. When substituting arrowroot for flour, use one-half as much arrowroot as you would flour.

artichoke

The immature flower head of a thistle-like plant characterized by overlapping outer leaves. Commonly called a *globe artichoke*, don't confuse this with the *Jerusalem artichoke* which isn't an artichoke at all, but the tuberous base of a sunflower—and it doesn't come from Jerusalem.

☀ **To prepare an artichoke:** Wash by holding the stem and plunging up and down in a bowl of water. Cut off about one inch from the top and cut the stem even with the base. Use scissors or kitchen shears to trim 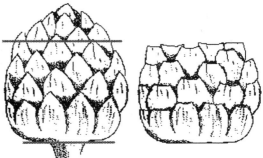 off the tops of the remaining leaves.

The furry choke in the center may be removed before cooking by spreading the leaves at the top and scraping it out with a spoon, then pressing the leaves back to return the artichoke to its original shape.

Dip in lemon juice or rub all of the cut edges with a piece of lemon to prevent discoloration. Place upright in a basket or trivet over an inch or two of boiling water, cover, and steam for about 40 minutes or until done.

Test for doneness by inserting the tip of a sharp knife into the base; when done, the knife should enter and exit easily. If the choke is not removed before cooking, place the artichoke in the pan top down and follow the cooking instructions above. Serve hot or cold.

Tip: Buy only artichokes with tightly closed leaves that are not discolored. Spreading leaves are a sign of an older artichoke that has passed its peak for flavor and tenderness.

* **Uncored artichoke:** The uncored artichoke should be served with melted butter, mayonnaise, Hollandaise or other sauce on the side so that the outer leaves can be removed individually and dipped. The leaf is then dragged through the teeth to extract the small edible portion at the base. When the small, yellowish leaves that surround the choke appear, pull them out together with the choke. Remove any remaining fiber and cut up the heart of the artichoke to dip with a fork or toothpick.

* **Cored and stuffed artichoke:** As an individual serving or part of an antipasto, a cored artichoke can be filled with such things as Hollandaise sauce, mayonnaise, cocktail shrimp, carrots or peas in cream sauce, or vegetables marinated in salad dressing.

Artichoke—Filled with dipping sauce after removing choke

asparagus

Fresh asparagus looks so inviting, but how do you fit those long spears in a pan? Tradition calls for tying them into a bundle, then standing them upright in a tall, narrow pan designed specifically for that purpose or in a makeshift cooker comprised of two saucepans, one inverted over the other. Fortunately, there are alternatives.

Tip: Buy asparagus with tight green buds. Buds that are pulling away from the stems, discoloration, and wilting are all signs of aging or of a vegetable that has been mishandled.

- **Preparation:** Good asparagus requires little cooking, but no amount of cooking will tenderize woody stems or asparagus that is old. Trim about one inch off the base of the stems; if they are thick, trim the woody outer part with a vegetable peeler or paring knife. Note that smaller or younger stalks may require little or no trimming.
- **Cooking I:** Stalks can be cut in half or in uniform lengths and placed in a basket or trivet for steaming, covered, over about one inch of boiling water. If whole spears are preferred, use a large frying pan or bamboo steamer.

  Cooking time will vary with the thickness of the stalk and doneness desired, but should average about ten minutes.
- **Cooking II:** Stir frying is a quicker and often tastier alternative for young, fresh cut asparagus—simply place the pieces in a hot, oiled wok or frying pan, stir often, and remove when desired doneness is reached.
- **Garnish:** Asparagus thrives on simple garnishes such as melted butter, buttered bread crumbs, or a sprinkling of Parmesan cheese. Cold asparagus goes well with mayonnaise. For color, garnish with strips of pimiento, orange peel, lemon peel, or chopped tomato.

aspic

A clear gelatin commonly flavored with stock, wine, etc., used as a glaze or a mold for seafood, meat, vegetables, or fruit.

To prepare stock for aspic, see *clarify*.

au gratin

We tend to associate *au gratin* with cheese, but in cookery, *gratin* actually refers to the thin top crust formed when a dish is browned in the oven or under a broiler. The crust is commonly formed by a topping of finely crushed dry bread crumbs, or a combination of bread crumbs and butter or cheese. Some toppings call for crushed crackers, crushed corn flakes, or even finely ground nuts.

avocado

A native American fruit, pear-shaped, with a thick skin, large pit and nut-like flavor. There are two types normally available: one with a smooth, light green skin and one with a pebbled, dark green skin. The avocado does not take kindly to heat and is usually served cold in combination with citrus fruit, shrimp, crab meat, or in a dip.

A ripe avocado will yield slightly to pressure on the surface of the skin. Use ripe, firm avocados for salad or garnish; softer ones for dip. An unripe avocado will ripen slowly at room temperature or more quickly if placed in a paper bag.

To slice the avocado, cut completely around the fruit, top to bottom, through to the pit. Take one half in each hand and twist to separate the fruit from the pit. Remove the peel, slice if desired, and immediately coat all exposed portions with lemon juice to avoid discoloration.

Tip: To save an unused portion of avocado, leave the pit in, cover the exposed surfaces with a thin coat of butter or mayonnaise and wrap tightly in foil. Do not freeze.

avocado dip (guacamole)

There are all sorts of variations for this dish, so vary the ingredients to suit your taste. Here's one to get you started:

- Prepare a very ripe avocado as above, mash with a fork, and blend with one small finely-chopped tomato, one small grated onion, one tablespoon of chili powder (more or less to taste), one teaspoon olive oil, one teaspoon lime or lemon juice, and one-quarter teaspoon coriander. Salt and pepper to taste. Serve immediately.

Guacamole may be served as an appetizer dip with tortilla chips or a spread for crackers. It may also be used as a filling for tacos or a garnish for meat or fish.

Tip: If made ahead, put the avocado seed in the spread and wrap tightly to avoid discoloring. Any darkening of the surface does not indicate spoilage; it just looks unappetizing and can be easily removed before serving.

avocado salad

There are probably as many variations of avocado salad as there are of guacamole. Almost all begin with a bed of lettuce leaves or shredded lettuce. Generally, allow half an avocado per serving or use slices as garnish. The avocado half can be left in one piece and used as a small bowl to hold chicken salad, tuna salad, small shrimp, citrus fruit, etc. Or each half can be cut into wedges or thin slices and arranged decoratively on a plate along with the other ingredients. Garnish with sprouts and decoratively cut vegetables.

bacon

Despite its unsavory reputation as coming from "the part of the pig that went over the fence last" (although it really doesn't—bacon is cut from the back or side of the hog), or in recent years, as a carrier of deadly cholesterol, we still refer to making a living or succeeding at some endeavor as "bringing home the bacon." Most of us prefer to see it in the latter light, as something special. Salted and flavored by the wood over which it is smoked, all varieties are distinctive and some are even famous. Fear of hardening our arteries keeps us from consuming copious quantities at breakfast as in the past, but it only takes a little bacon to add a wonderful flavoring to many dishes.

bagel

A doughnut-shaped roll with a chewy texture, made by dropping plain yeast dough briefly into hot water before baking. Traditionally a breakfast treat served with cream cheese or lox, bagels are increasingly replacing bread or rolls in sandwiches.

bagna cauda See *anchovy*

baguette

A long, round, tapered loaf of French bread.
Baguettes are the perfect size for making toasted rounds for canapés or for served with soup or salad.

Tip: For serving sandwiches to a crowd, make them from whole baguette loaves and slice into serving-sized pieces. If sandwiches are made ahead, don't add tomato until just before serving; liquid from the tomatoes will make the sandwiches soggy and they contain enzymes that soften other foods, especially cheese, as well.

bake

Baking is essentially the cooking of food by dry heat, usually in an oven. Depending on what is being cooked, it can be a very exacting or a very forgiving process.

Oven temperature, timing, and even positioning on the oven shelf are critical when baking foods such as biscuits, bread, and cakes that must rise, or custard that must set.

Many preparations such as lasagna, scalloped potatoes, and meat dishes are covered and cooked partly by the dry heat of the oven and partly by the moist heat of liquid released from the food. Here the temperature and even timing are not so critical, although lower heat will of course increase the cooking time. In fact, most such dishes can be "baked" on top of the stove as long as the bottom of the pan is shielded from direct heat to prevent scorching.

baked Alaska

A dessert comprised of ice cream enclosed in sponge or angel cake and covered with meringue. The tricky part is to brown the meringue quickly under a broiler without melting the ice cream.

baked beans

Generally, in the U.S., *baked beans* refers to navy, northern or pinto beans flavored with tomato sauce, molasses, meat and a variety of spices, then baked for hours in a low oven.

Simply stated, baked beans are beans mixed with other stuff and baked to heat them through and blend the flavors—but that description hardly does justice to their culinary or nutritional attributes. Throughout the world, a wide variety of beans are combined with a host of other ingredients and then baked or cooked over heat in some similar fashion.

Nutritionally, beans are a rich source of soluble fiber purported to lower blood cholesterol, and insoluble fiber which aids digestion. See also, **beans**.

baking powder

A combination of dry acid and alkaline ingredients that in the presence of moisture form carbon dioxide; used as a leavening agent that causes batter or dough to rise.

There are different types of baking powder; double-acting is the most stable and thus the most commonly used today.

baking soda

If you have ever tasted a cake made by someone who mistakenly used baking soda instead of baking powder you won't soon forget it. Needless to say, they aren't the same.

Baking soda, an alkaline (see **baking powder**, above), needs the help of an acid ingredient such as buttermilk in order to act as a leavening agent.

Most recipes that call for baking soda in addition to baking powder require the baking soda to neutralize acid from certain ingredients while the baking powder provides the leavening action.

Far outdistancing its use in cookery is the application of baking soda as a cleanser and to absorb odors in the refrigerator, garbage disposal, etc.

baklava

A Greek pastry made of **phyllo** stuffed with chopped nuts and coated with honey.

baller

Also called a **melon baller**, a kitchen utensil used to cut decorative balls from melons and other fruit.

bamboo shoots

The tender, young shoots from an edible bamboo plant. Used extensively in oriental cooking, they are most often available canned and may be used to compliment most meat dishes or stuffed for serving as hors d'oeuvres.

bamboo steamer

If you missed the ads on late-night TV, there's hope for you yet, because this handiest of all kitchen utensils is available in most  kitchen supply stores at very afford-able prices. Most are two-tiered, but they may be three- or four-tiered.

Position the steamer over a *wok* or large fry pan containing an inch or so of barely simmering water and you have a versatile multi-tiered cooker. Place chicken, fish, or vegetables on a sheet of foil to steam them; heat leftovers in their storage containers; or heat dinner right on the plate, but be careful, because the plate gets hot too. Avoid the hot steam by removing the steamer tray from over the heat before removing the lid.

Tip: Use plates slightly smaller than the steamer tray to allow the steam to pass through to those above. Serve the food using the tray as a holder for the hot plate.

banana

A tropical fruit widely available in the U.S. that is an excellent source of potassium. Bananas will ripen at room temperature, but you can forget that old saw about never putting them in the refrigerator: they can be refrigerated after they are ripe—the skin darkens, but the flesh will remain firm and fresh for several days. Bananas combine well with most other fruit and nuts. Serve a mixture of banana slices, orange wedges, grapes, etc. topped with salad dressing as a unique first course, or with sweet syrup as a dessert or palate cleanser after seafood.

Tip: Toss banana slices in a little lemon or lime juice to keep them from darkening.

bananas Foster

A classic dessert comprising bananas that have been sautéed in a mixture of butter, brown sugar and rum, then served with the syrup resulting from cooking, usually over ice cream.

banana smoothie

A thick, delicious combination of bananas, milk, and honey combined in a blender. Ice cubes may be added to thin and chill the mixture, and it can be enhanced with other flavorings such as a little vanilla, cinnamon or yogurt. If you want to be really decadent, try a little chocolate syrup!

Tip: Store over-ripe bananas in the freezer and use them for smoothies or to flavor muffins, cakes, custard or sherbet.

barbecue or barbeque

A method of dry-heat cooking. The term is said by some to come from the Spanish *barbacoa,* a wooden or metal rack that holds meat for cooking or smoking; others trace it back to early French settlers who cooked local goats *barbe à queue,* or beard to tail.

We certainly don't want to throw cold water on a pleasant summer afternoon of grilling hamburgers beard to tail, but there are a couple of simple precautions to consider:

- As die-hard fans of the flavor that attests to food having been cooked over an open wood fire, we're not inclined to recommend any hi-tech instruments, except one: a meat thermometer, in order to be sure that hamburger and chicken have been brought to the proper temperature to destroy harmful bacteria.
- Also, watch the food and turn it often to avoid charring: the carbon thus formed has been cited as a carcinogen. (Then again, what hasn't?)

On a more pleasant note, to cook vegetables on the barbecue without the bother of skewers, try these tricks:

- Onions, peppers, or tomatoes can be wrapped whole or cut up in foil with a bit of butter, salt, and pepper. Great flavor!
- Potatoes with the skins on, sliced thick, can be placed directly on the grill until they brown. For faster results, parboil or bake the whole potatoes first, but only until they begin to soften.
- To barbecue fresh corn, pull back the husk from the top to remove the silk, push the husk back to cover the corn, dip the ears in cold water, and place them on the grill. The corn will steam in the husk

barley

A grain used as animal feed, in the making of malt...and for soup. Barley soup is favored in other parts of the world, but doesn't seem to have caught on in the U.S. We're inclined to go with the crowd on this one, although barley is a hearty addition to a vegetable soup.

basil

A fragrant herb that is at its best fresh and finely chopped, sprinkled over a plate of vine-ripened, sliced tomatoes that have been lightly salted. In fact, fresh basil is a welcome addition to almost any cold salad.

In addition, it is difficult to imagine Italian tomato sauce, cooked vegetable dishes such as *ratatouille*, or any number of meat dishes without the kiss of basil, fresh or dried.

By the way, basil is an easy plant to grow in order to keep a fresh supply readily at hand and as a special bonus, some varieties impart a delightful minty scent throughout the area where they grow.

baste

To moisten food, usually meat, while it is cooking.

The moistener may consist of melted butter, a sauce, or the juice in which the food is cooking. A *baster* is often used, although the liquid can just as easily be spooned over.

baster

A kitchen device consisting of a tube of plastic or metal with a flexible bulb at one end. Squeezing the bulb and then releasing it while the end is immersed draws liquid up into the tube, allowing it to be released over cooking food or into another container.

Tip: To separate fat from the juices in a pan, pour the liquid into a clear measuring cup or other container; allow the fat to rise to the top and use a baster to extract the liquid from beneath it.

batter

Generally, any semi-liquid mixture of flour with milk or water that may contain other ingredients as well, used to make pancakes, waffles, muffins, etc. A batter often contains egg to bind it, baking powder for leavening, and spices or other flavoring.

bay leaf

Used extensively in stews, soups, stuffing and marinades, this aromatic leaf is an essential flavor in French cuisine.

Bay leaf also adds zest to Italian tomato sauce, but be sparing in its use, for a little goes a long way.

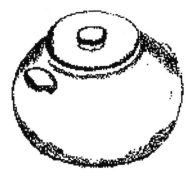

bean pot
Designed for slow cooking with a minimum loss of moisture, traditional bean pots are fat and rounded with tightly fitted lids.

beans
Beans, or legumes comprise a family of plants that produce seeds enclosed in a pod that enter into our diet in a multitude of ways, from snap beans, wax beans, and their many cousins that are eaten with the hull or pod to those seeds of the pea family (including several described in the next paragraph) that are normally eaten without the hull unless they are very young and tender.

Of the varieties of hulled beans generally available to us—lima, kidney, navy, northern, kidney, butter, black, black-eyed peas, and garbanzos, to list a few—all have a distinctive flavor and character. They tend to mix well with each other (you have to experiment with combinations to find out which you like), and with most other vegetables, meats, and even fruit. One hardly need consult a recipe: beans can be added to a meat casserole to flavor and extend it; conversely, leftovers can be used to flavor a bean dish.

In addition to providing a savory dish, these beans carry nutritional rewards: served with a small amount of meat or rice, they comprise a complete protein and the soluble fiber in the beans has been directly linked to a lowering of blood cholesterol. The soybean, from which tofu is made, has become popular as a filler or meat substitute in prepared foods because it provides a complete protein coupled with a low fat content.

bean sprout
The germinating or sprouting plant of the mung, alfalfa or other seed. Sprouting significantly increases the normally high vitamin content of the seed and provides a tasty addition to salads, soups, stir-fry and other dishes.

An ever-widening variety of sprouts are becoming available in the supermarket, and seeds can also be sprouted easily at home. Check out a health food store for organic seeds—most have directions right on the package.

Béarnaise Sauce

A classic sauce of vinegar that has been boiled with white wine seasoned with tarragon, shallots, chervil, parsley and pepper, then combined with egg yolks and melted butter. Béarnaise is especially good over broiled red meat, but may also be served with fish.

beat

Batter, described above, probably gets its name from the way in which it is made—by beating or 'battering' it.

In contrast to that traditional designation, mixing or beating is something of an art. Most recipes will be quite specific about the way in which ingredients are to be combined, but here are a few tips to help you along:

To **cream** is to combine ingredients such as butter and sugar with the hands or with the back of a (preferably) wooden spoon against the side of a bowl without excess motion so as to avoid inducing air into the mixture or breaking it down.

To **stir** or **blend**, use a circular motion without lifting the spoon or whisk from the bottom of the bowl. This combines the ingredients without inducing air into the mixture.

Tip: When a recipe for pancakes or muffins advises mixing just to combine ingredients, be sure to do so. Grit your teeth, ignore the lumps and you will be rewarded with a lighter, fluffier product.

To **beat** or **whip**, stir from top to bottom in order to bring ingredients up from the bottom and to trap air in the mixture. An electric mixer is excellent for this operation.

Tip: For whipping egg whites or cream by hand, beat vigorously with a whisk until the mixture begins to thicken. then continue to beat with less intensity just to trap more air in the mixture. And be careful to mix just enough—you will be amazed at how quickly egg whites are transformed from the soft peak stage to stiff, or whipped cream turned into butter!

To **fold** is to combine ingredients with a minimum of disruption. Normally ordered when making a mixture lighter by the addition of whipped cream, beaten egg whites, etc., the idea is to blend the ingredients without decreasing the bulk.

béchamel

Those of us fond of sauces could not exist without béchamel or cream sauce as it is the base for so many favorites.

To make a basic white sauce, prepare a *roux* by melting two tablespoons of butter over low heat, then blending in two tablespoons of flour and continuing to stir the mixture over the heat without browning for about three minutes to get rid of the raw flour taste. Off the heat, slowly stir in one cup of milk and, when it is completely combined, return the mixture to the heat. Cook and stir until the mixture is thickened and smooth. Season to taste with salt and white pepper. A dash of cayenne pepper or nutmeg will further enhance the flavor.

Herbs, spices, and a host of other ingredients may be added, depending on how the sauce is to be served. Use this sauce to make creamed spinach, corn, carrots, or peas. Add cheese, chopped tomatoes, mushrooms, or scallions and serve over toast, pasta, or chicken. Add a little tarragon or dill to serve over fish.

For a thicker sauce, increase the amount of flour and butter in proportion to the liquid. For a richer sauce, use cream in place of milk. And if you are counting fat and calories, margarine or olive oil may be substituted for the butter, and vegetable water or bouillon substituted for the milk.

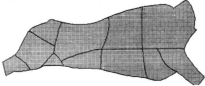

beef

In *The American Frugal Housewife*, the author tells us that the chuck is a very good piece of meat and that it is cheap, costing from four to five cents a pound. Sounds inexpensive even though the book was published about 150 years ago!

Concerns about cholesterol have caused most of us to reduce the amount of beef we consume, but it has by no means been driven off the menu. A couple of things to keep in mind when buying beef:

- Well-marbled beef is generally more tender than a leaner cut, but is inclined to be less flavorful.
- Leaner cuts of beef must be served *very* rare or *very* well done if they are to be tender.

Beef Bourguignonne
A traditional French stew of beef that is marinated in red wine then cooked in the marinade with shallots and mushrooms.

Beef Stroganoff
A dish comprising thin strips of beef in a sauce of mushrooms, white wine and sour cream.

Beef Wellington
A classic preparation of a roast of beef that has been coated with a liver pâté or paste and baked in a pastry shell.

beer

A beverage made from grain or from the extracts of roots or bark. Almost every country in the world has at least one local beer.
Beer that is produced from malted grain is generally fermented by yeast, flavored with hops, and contains 3% to 5% alcohol. There are fewer than 100 breweries in the U.S. compared to over 1,000 in Germany where local brews are common, although three of the most familiar terms associated with beer in this country come from towns in Czechoslovakia: Budweis, Micholup, and Pilsen (where the first pale lager was produced).
Beer made from roots or bark such as root beer, birch beer or ginger beer are non-alcoholic, sweetened, effervesced beverages.

beet
A red or white root vegetable with edible leaves. Beets are commonly served cooked, although they may be cut into julienne strips and served raw as a garnish.

Harvard beets
Sweet and sour beets made by cooking in a mixture of sugar, cornstarch, and mild vinegar seasoned with salt and cloves. Often served topped with a dab of butter or orange marmalade.

beet greens

Don't throw away those greens when you buy fresh beets! They are flavorful as well as a good source of fiber, potassium, and vitamin A.

Beet greens should be rinsed well to remove any grit They can then be steamed until tender in a frying pan lightly coated with butter or cooking oil using only the moisture that remains after rinsing.

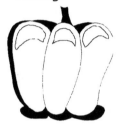

bell pepper

Any variety of large, mild pepper shaped somewhat like a bell that may be green, yellow or red in color.

Benedictine

A liqueur originally made by Benedictine monks, flavored with a secret combination of herbs.

biscuit

A type of quick bread made with baking powder and shaped with a cutter, cut into squares or strips with a knife, or dropped by the spoonful onto a baking sheet.

For variety:

- Incorporate flavoring agents such as cheese, bacon, parsley, or chives into the dough.
- Dust biscuits with a mixture of cinnamon and sugar or Parmesan cheese.
- Stuff biscuits: roll a section of dough to half the normal thickness; top with a filling of berries, chopped dried fruit or ground cooked meat; top with a second thin layer of dough and crimp the edges; then cut into squares before baking.

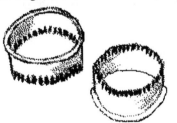

biscuit cutter

Biscuit or round pastry cutters are available in a variety of sizes with smooth or crinkled edges. In addition to cutting pastry, they can be used for a variety of other tasks, such as cutting uniform rounds from vegetable slices or aspic, coring slices of fresh pineapple, or cutting ravioli.

bisque

As with many terms, the precise definition of *bisque* has gone through a series of transformations throughout the last two centuries. In the present day, authoritative sources describe a bisque as a thick, rich soup that has as its base a purée of shellfish (especially crayfish) combined with cream. In general use, however, we have noted a tendency to use the term for any purée and cream soup base that is delicately spiced.

black beans

About the size and shape of kidney beans and of course black in color, black beans seem to be used mainly for soup in Puerto Rican and Cuban cuisines, although a thicker variation prepared with onions, peppers and garlic often crops up as a side dish with rice.

black-eyed pea

An appropriate name for a white pea with a black spot on it and certainly more appealing than its earlier designation as a cowpea. This delicious vegetable, like grits, has long been considered a southern dish although it is gaining in popularity on tables north of the Mason-Dixon line.

black pepper

A popular condiment ground from the tiny dried fruit of an East Indian plant.

blackthorn

A thorny, deciduous Eurasian shrub having white flowers and small, bluish-black, plum-like fruits used chiefly for flavoring alcoholic beverages such as sloe gin. Also called *sloe*.

black walnut

The rich, oily meat of a nut similar in form to the more common English walnut and the pecan.

blanching

Any of a variety of techniques that use boiling water to process or cook foods:

❀ One type of blanching, used to rid certain meats of excess salt or strong flavor, involves covering with cold water, bringing the water to a boil and simmering for the time specified in the recipe, then plunging the meat quickly in cold water to arrest the cooking.

❋ Another type calls for adding fruit or vegetables to boiling water briefly as a first step to canning or freezing, or for a longer period to cook through completely.

❋ A third type is the technique of pouring boiling water over such foods as tomatoes, peaches, or almonds so as to soften the skins and make them easier to remove.

blancmange

A flavored and sweetened milk pudding thickened with cornstarch.

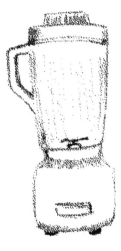

blender

A kitchen appliance comprising a glass, metal, or plastic container having a set of blades at the bottom and that sits on a motorized base containing on, off, and speed control settings.

Blenders often come with a variety of attachments so that the differences between them and the *food processor* or *mixer* may be somewhat obscured.

The blender is extremely convenient for preparing purées, soups, batters, and beverages. Some include a smaller container with sturdier blades for milling coffee, chopping ice, and processing lesser quantities such as for nuts or herbs.

When purchasing a blender:

• Look for a two-piece top that makes it convenient to add ingredients without spattering.

• Consider whether you want a container that allows viewing the food as it processes—consistency can change dramatically in moments.

• Find one with a removable bottom for ease in emptying the container and in cleaning the blades

• Decide whether a model featuring twenty speeds is really worth the money—a convenient on-off switch is adequate for most needs.

See also, *pastry blender.*

bleu cheese or blue cheese

A strong cheese similar to Roquefort that gets its name from the bluish mold running through it; commonly served with crackers as an appetizer or with fruit at the end of a meal.

Those who enjoy creamy bleu cheese dressing may be pleasantly surprised by the delicious and less calorie-laden alternative of mixing bits of bleu cheese with a good oil and vinegar dressing (with the possible addition of a pinch of sugar to cut the acidity).

Forced by inclement weather to move a barbecue indoors years ago, we created **Bleu Cheese Steak** in our quest for a more flavorful oven-broiled steak. After broiling the steaks, spread butter, crumbled bleu cheese and a liberal sprinkling of paprika on a heavy platter. Place the platter in the oven just long enough to melt and blend the ingredients, then place each of the steaks in turn on the hot platter to coat them. Serve immediately.

blini

Thin pancakes similar to *crêpes,* traditionally served with sour cream and caviar.

blintz

A thin pancake similar to a *crêpe*, stuffed with a cottage cheese mixture and often topped with fruit and sour cream.

Bloody Mary

A cocktail made with vodka and tomato juice.

The traditional Bloody Mary was one part vodka to two parts juice with a healthy dose of Worcestershire, a dash of lemon juice, a couple drops of Tabasco, and salt & pepper. These days it is usually a tall drink (lots more tomato juice) with emphasis on the hot sauce and a colorful garnish such as a stick of carrot or celery.

blue laws

Originally, a reference to local ordinances that prohibited a variety of activities on Sunday. Now generally used in reference to restrictions on business, such as of retail stores, restaurants, etc. especially regarding the serving of alcoholic beverages on Sunday.

blue plate special

A restaurant meal served at a special price.

boil
In cooking, to bring liquid to the temperature at which it begins to vaporize into steam, or to cook in a liquid so heated.

bolster
The part of a knife connecting the handle and the blade. See *cutlery.*

bonbon
A candy, usually chocolate covered and cream filled.

bone, debone
To remove the bones, as from a fish or fowl.

borsch, borscht, borsht

A soup of beets and cabbage made with beef stock and served with sour cream. Borsch may be served hot or cold.

Boston baked beans
Among the numerous combinations that comprise bean dishes (see *beans*) are those that claim to be *Boston baked.* More aptly described as *New England style,* the multitude of recipes do have a few things in common: only navy beans are used and purists insist on starting with dried beans; they must be prepared with salt pork; most of the sweetening and flavoring comes from molasses with an assist from brown sugar; and they require a *bean pot* in which the beans are baked at a moderate temperature for up to eight hours.

bottle brush
A long handled brush with bristles extending straight out at a 90° angle from the sides, that may range in size from about one-quarter inch to over two inches in diameter.

bottle opener
The bottle opener most familiar is the one used to pry the pressure cap off a narrow-necked bottle. In addition, there are a variety of devices for unscrewing lids, from rubber pads that improve one's grip, to hinged affairs that look like misshapen nutcrackers, to tapered flanges that are installed under a cabinet or shelf, to an elaborate tool with an adjustable steel band that encircles the lid.

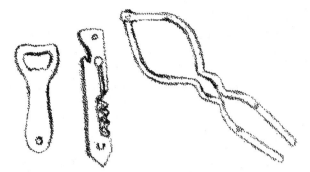

Tip: There are lots of ways to loosen a stubborn bottle or jar cap; here's one from a friend of ours—set the container down with a bit of force squarely and sharply on a flat surface. It really works!

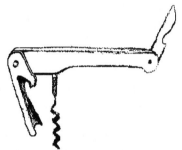

For opening corked bottles, there are a variety of devices such as the "waiter's friend" pictured above or combination openers that screw into the cork and then remove it by turning a second screw or raising a pair of handles (see *corkscrew*).

botulism

Illness caused by toxins produced in foods that have been improperly canned or preserved. Botulism is especially insidious because there are often no signs of its presence. The disease is manifested in stomach pains followed by difficulty with vision; a physician should be consulted as soon as symptoms appear.

The best defense is, of course, prevention. Avoid any suspect foods, such as those that smell off or show signs of fermentation, however slight. Home-canned vegetables should be boiled for a minimum of fifteen minutes before serving; meat, five to seven minutes longer.

bouillabaisse

A fish stew made with a broth of water or white wine and flavored mainly with tomatoes, garlic and saffron.

There are a number of regional variations on this dish, but a true bouillabaisse can only be made near the Mediterranean, for some of the fish required are available only there and they do not ship well.

bouillon

A stock or broth; generally, the liquid in a stockpot. Don't confuse this with the stuff on the grocer's shelf that should rightfully be labeled *'Salt With A Little Flavoring'*.

We don't often have the time to prepare a home-made broth, but it is worth trying now and then as with the left-over carcass of a Thanksgiving turkey. Place the bones and other inedible portions (except the liver) in a large pot of water on a back burner of the stove; add some spices (basil, bay leaf, thyme, sage), salt, and pepper; and allow it to simmer for a day or two, adding vegetable trimmings (especially those from tomatoes, onions, and celery) as they become available. Taste from time to time and, if necessary, allow it to boil down to concentrate the flavor. Strain the stock and you have broth. If you *clarify* the stock, it will keep for months in the freezer.

Similarly, an accumulation of aging vegetables or vegetable cuttings can be used to make a vegetable broth although the cooking time will be shorter.

Note that home-made stock is not just for soup; a flavorful stock is the perfect base for a sauce.

Tip: Freeze stock in an ice cube tray and bag the cubes for easy access when you need only a small amount of stock.

Another Tip: Avoid root vegetable such as potatoes in the stock as they tend to sour if the cooking time is long.

bouquet garni

A collection of herbs such as parsley, basil, bay leaf, thyme, rosemary, and sage that are added to soups and stocks. Makeup of the bouquet will vary depending on the dish. Fresh herbs are best, but dried will do. The *bouquet garni* is removed before the dish is served. Fresh herbs can be tied together in a **faggot**, whereas dried herbs will require wrapping in cheesecloth for easy removal.

bourbon

An American whiskey distilled from at least 51% corn mash at a maximum of 180 proof and aged at least two years in new charred oak barrels.

bowl

To most, a bowl is any deep rounded container. To the serious cook, each bowl requires at least one adjective to distinguish it from the others. And we don't confuse *bowls* with *storage containers*.

In general, avoid those cute sets of half a dozen bowls in graduated sizes, especially if they are plastic. You will most likely use and reuse one or two while the rest gather dust. Better to buy two or three bowls in sizes that you regularly use.

Composition, or the material from which the bowl is made depends on how you use it. If you want a bowl that is easily turned or held off the counter top for whipping egg whites, cream, or omelets quickly, look for lightweight metal and a smoothly rounded shape. If you mix egg whites often, a copper bowl that reacts chemically to produce a tighter mixture might be considered, although they are expensive—looks good hanging on the wall, too. For breads, batters, stuffing, and the like get a heavier glass or ceramic bowl that won't move around as easily as a light bowl. Plastic should be avoided as it tends to retain oils even after washing.

Size depends on what you do and in what volume. Have at least one oversized bowl that allows tossing a salad easily, or whipping eggs or cream without decorating the walls.

Shape is also important. The sides should slope without sharp breaks that serve only to collect food that can't be reached with a whisk.

Tip: As to the matter of storage, use square containers with tight-fitiing lids: they take less room in the refrigerator or freezer, the lids keep the contents fresh, and you won't have to go looking for the mixing or serving bowls when you need them.

boysenberry

A large, dark red berry that is a cross between varieties of raspberry and blackberry.

braise

A moist heat method for cooking less tender cuts of meat with a little liquid in a tightly-lidded pan.

Meat is usually browned, then placed in a pan to which about a half-inch of water, broth, or other cooking liquid is added. Once the liquid is brought to a boil on top of the stove, the heat is reduced to allow the liquid to simmer. Cooking can be completed on top of the stove or the pan may be placed in the oven heated to about 300°.

bran

The husk that is normally separated from grain before it is ground into flour.

brand, brand name

The symbol or name by which a product is known. Although a brand name does not guarantee quality, it may denote consistency, giving the buyer a means to identify preferred products.

brandy

A fine liquor distilled from grape wine.

A brandy that has been distilled from fruit other than grapes is so noted on the label, such as *apricot brandy* that is distilled from fermented apricots and is called a *fruit brandy* that should not be confused with a *fruit-flavored brandy* which is brandy to which fruit flavoring has been added.

Brandy is made throughout the world, wherever wine is made, but two areas stand out—*Cognac* and *Armagnac* designate brandy made in those districts in France, and only brandy made in those districts should carry their respective names.

brasier, brazier
A cooking appliance consisting of a charcoal or electric heat source over which food is grilled.

bratwurst
A well-seasoned sausage usually served fried. Bratwurst is traditionally made from pork, but in the U.S. commonly available made from beef.

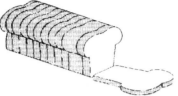

bread
It is not surprising that "bread-winner" designates one who supports and feeds a family, as bread in one form or another is a part of virtually every cuisine.

Bread may be defined as dough made of flour and water, fermented and baked. Unfortunately, this description excludes the wonderful varieties of unleavened breads and those that are cooked in some other manner popularized in various parts of the world, such as tortillas, Scandinavian flat bread, American Indian fry bread, and even English muffins which are cooked by frying!

Tip: Attesting to the good feeling that bread gives us is a Realtor's suggestion for placing a slice of bread in a warm oven to create a pleasant aroma when showing a house. Works great for company as well!

breadboard
❧ A flat surface, often smooth marble, on which bread and pastries are mixed and rolled out. Also called a *pastry board*.

✦ A flat surface, often wood, on which bread is sliced and often served.

✦ See also, *cutting board*.

bread box

A container for storing bread, usually of metal or lined with metal, designed to keep the bread fresh.

Tip: An earthenware crock tall enough to hold a loaf of bread and with a loose-fitting lid can also provide excellent storage. The main thing to remember is that the container should be ventilated to prevent molding while keeping the crust crisp.

bread crumbs

Fragments of bread used in food preparation. Be sure to follow recipe directions for the type of breadcrumbs required:

- **Dry crumbs** are made from stale or dried bread. Bread can be crumbed with a hand grater, a blender, or by placing the bread in a plastic bag and crushing it with a rolling pin, the bottom of a sturdy glass, the flat of a knife, or any other implement at hand.

- **Soft crumbs** are prepared from bread that has not completely dried out and may be crumbled in the hand or by pulling the bread apart with a fork, taking care not to crush the bread in the process.

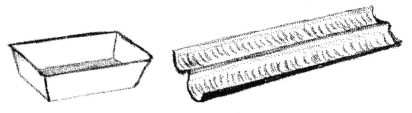

bread pan

An open container in which bread is baked.

In addition to conventional rectangular loaf pans, there are round loaf pans, *brioche* pans that are fluted and sloped outward from the base, French *baguette* tins similar to the one pictured above on the right that are half-round metal strips designed to hold two strips of soft dough, and others. Some breads are baked directly on a cookie sheet or an oven stone.

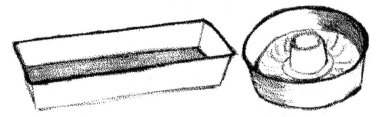

For variety, bread can be baked in a long pan or tube tin, both pictured above, or as individual loaves baked in small loaf pans or large muffin tins.

brewer's yeast

☀ A type of yeast used in the brewing of beer.

☀ The yeast that is left after the brewing process is completed, also called *debittered brewer's yeast* or *nutritional yeast*.

Although it's leavening qualities are gone, this yeast has great nutritional value. Added in modest quantity to such foods as bread, soup, dressings, etc. it has little effect on taste and none on texture.

Nutritional yeast can be used as a coating for fried or baked tofu, mushrooms, eggplant, and other mild-flavored foods. It imparts a very pleasant flavor that changes with the method and length of time cooked.

brick cheese

A semi-soft American cheese.

brie

A delicately flavored soft cheese with a reddish-white crust. When the cheese is properly aged, the crust is edible and imparts a special flavor of its own that blends with the cheese.

brine

A solution of water and salt, often spiced, used to preserve and flavor foods.

brioche
A light rich bread often baked as a round and stuffed with a sweet or savory preparation.

brisket
Stew meat cut from the breast of an animal.

brisling
* A sprat; a small marine food fish of northeast Atlantic waters that is eaten fresh or smoked and is often canned in oil as a sardine.
* Any of various similar fishes, such as a young herring

broccoli
A plant of the cabbage family with delicate green flower stalks that mass together to form a head.

Broccoli, rich in vitamin C and carotene, has been touted as a cancer preventive.

brochette
The skewer on which pieces of meat or vegetable are impaled for barbecuing or broiling.

broil
Generally, the process of cooking quickly by exposing food to extreme heat, such as that of an open flame, top heat from an oven burner, or in a heavy, heated pan.

Broiling is used to top-brown certain dishes covered with sauce, cheese, or bread crumbs, and to cook meats. Broiling of meat should be accomplished in a relatively short period of time so as not to dry out or toughen the flesh; meats such as chicken that are to be cooked through should be cut or pounded thin.

Tip: The practice of leaving the oven door ajar when broiling to prevent the oven from shutting down as the temperature rises is generally not necessary, but is, nevertheless, a good practice in order to watch the cooking, as food under the broiler seems to make a rapid transition from raw to charred.

broiler

* A kitchen appliance or a part of the oven used for broiling.
* A chicken that is suitable for broiling, that is, one small enough to cook through without burning the outside.

broth

A clear *stock* made by cooking meat, vegetables or cereal in water. See also, *bouillon*.

brown

The process of cooking in a frying pan or under a broiler until food has lost its natural color and turns brown, usually to seal in the natural juices.

brown rice

Rice that has not been processed or *polished*, that is, rice with the germ and bran intact. Brown rice is nutritionally superior to white rice although it generally requires longer cooking.

brown sauce

Any of the classic sauces such as Demi-Glace, Sauce Españole, or the Tomato Sauces (not to be confused with Italian sauce traditionally served over pasta) that form the base for a number of other sauces. Some, such as sauce Españole, require many hours of careful preparation, although, fortunately, acceptable substitutes may be made from commercial ingredients.

brown sugar

Sugar which gets its characteristic color (light or dark brown) from the addition of molasses that are produced in the refining process.

Brussels sprouts

Like miniature heads of cabbage, another member of that family, high in vitamin C and a reputed cancer inhibitor.

Although commonly served with butter and perhaps a bit of salt as the obligatory green vegetable, Brussels sprouts take well to flavored white sauces such as of curry or cheese.

Cold dilled or curried Brussels sprouts are made by tossing sprouts that have cooled with sour cream or yogurt flavored with dill weed or curry powder. Serve as a side dish or to garnish a salad plate.

bun

Where you are from determines whether a bun is a dinner roll, a sweet roll, or both. In any case, buns are usually uniform in size and light of texture, made from yeasted bread dough.

burgundy

Originally designating the wines of the Burgundy region in France, the term has come to be used to describe a variety of full-bodied, dry, red or white wines that are similar to burgundy.

butter

- A fatty condiment derived from the milk of mammals.
- Any of a number of elegant condiments, made to accompany the food being served, created by mixing dairy butter with such things as pureed anchovies, chives, crabmeat, crayfish, garlic, lemon rind, parsley, shallots, shrimp, or tarragon.
- Descriptive of a variety of products similar to dairy butter, but derived from other sources, such as *apple butter, cocoa butter,* or *peanut butter.*

butter bean

Strictly speaking, any light colored bean including lima, wax or fava. In our lexicon, however, the butter bean is a flat, tender, yellowish-white bean that looks like an oversized lima bean.

buttermilk

For those who reside in dairy country, buttermilk is the liquid left after the butter has been churned. For the rest of us, alas, it is a commercial preparation of fermented milk.

cabbage

A family of vegetables that includes broccoli, Brussels sprouts, cauliflower, kohlrabi, red cabbage, and white cabbage.

That which we commonly call cabbage is a vegetable made up of large green leaves that grow tightly together to form a head. Served raw in a salad or slaw, or cooked with butter or a cream sauce, green cabbage has a pleasant, distinctive flavor.

Tip: Cooking cabbage creates an odor that even many a cabbage lover finds offensive—a small dish of vinegar set out in the kitchen will absorb the aroma.

cacao

The seeds of a tropical American tree from which cocoa and chocolate are extracted.

Caesar salad

A salad of lettuce, anchovies, croutons and grated cheese blessed with a dressing of vinegar, olive oil, garlic, lemon juice and beaten egg.

Often the egg is omitted in deference to those who have reservations about consuming them raw.

café au lait

A coffee made by combining equal parts of strong black coffee and heated milk.

café royale

Hot black coffee served with a brandy-soaked cube of sugar on a teaspoon. The spoon is held over the cup, the brandy is ignited and, when it burns out, the contents of the spoon are added to the coffee.

caffeine

A stimulant naturally present in such substances as coffee, tea, and cola nuts.

cake

- ❋ A mixture of flour, eggs, sugar, milk, and leavening, baked and often served with a filling or a topping of sugar icing, pastry cream, pudding, or fruit.
- ❋ A small mass or patty of food that is baked or fried.

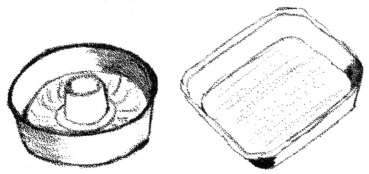

cake pan

Any of a diversity of rectangular, round, tube, or shaped pans used to hold cake batter for baking. Special pans are often used for the baking of traditional or ritual cakes prepared for certain holidays.

cake rack

A wire rack on which bread or cake is placed to cool and dry after baking.

calorie

- ❋ The amount of energy needed to raise the temperature of one gram of water by one degree Celsius.
- ❋ A unit of heat used to express the energy-producing quality of food. Food energy is measured in one thousand calorie units called *kilocalories* which in common parlance we've shortened to *calories*, so don't get your hopes up if someone claims you can lose weight on a one million calorie diet!

Calvados

A French brandy distilled from apple cider.

Camembert

A soft cheese similar to ***brie*** that takes its name from the village in France where it originated.

Canadian bacon
Smoked pork that is not bacon, but a type of ham.

canapé
A rectangle of bread with the crust removed that may be toasted or fried and spread with a mixture of some type.

Although we tend to think of canapés strictly as appetizers, in classic cuisine they often accompany another dish, either plain or with a topping that compliments the dish.

Tip: For a unique touch, make canapés from bread slices that have been cut into interesting shapes with cookie cutters.

candle
In the world of food, *candling* refers to the process of examining eggs by placing them in front of a strong light, often a candle.

candy, candied
To *candy* or become *candied,* refers to cooking with sugar or to crystallize like sugar.

cane sugar
Sugar extracted from sugar cane. Sugar is also commonly obtained from sugar beets.

cane syrup
The concentrated sap obtained from sugar cane. Although cane syrup is occasionally used to replace sugar, it is less sweet, so that more must be used as a substitute and the liquids in a recipe must also be adjusted to allow for the liquid syrup.

canister
A small container used for storing coffee, tea, sugar, etc.

canned goods
Food preserved in air-tight cans.

cannelloni
Italian—pipes. A dish that is made by cooking thin sheets of pasta dough, stuffing them with any of a variety of preparations containing cheese, chopped meat, spinach, mushrooms, etc., then rolling the dough into a cylinder. The rolls are then baked with sauce and grated cheese.

cannoli
An Italian confection comprised of a sweet filling wrapped in pastry dough and deep-fried.

canola
An oil low in saturated fats, obtained from a plant of the same family as the cabbage.

can opener
Any of a number of devises, either manual or electric, designed to remove the top from a sealed can.

Tip: When shopping for a can opener, find one that is easy to disassemble and clean; the blade of a can opener is a natural trap for bits of food that can harbor harmful bacteria.

cantaloupe
A strain of muskmelon with rough skin and sweet, bright orange flesh. The cantaloupe makes a fine addition to a combination of other fruit, ice cream, or salad.

Cantaloupe and *prosciutto* are flavors that complement each other wonderfully well. Simply wrap a slice of prosciutto around a thin wedge of cantaloupe and serve as an appetizer or hors d'oeuvre.

caper
The tiny bud of the caper bush that is pickled in vinegar and used as a condiment.

For just the right flavor, they should not be confused with the larger pickled nasturtium seeds often sold as capers.

capon
A castrated rooster bred for its large breast and tender flesh.

carafe
A glass, metal, or earthenware container for serving water, wine, or coffee.

caramel
Burnt sugar used as a flavoring or to add color to certain foods. Also used to describe a confection flavored with burnt sugar.

caramelize
To turn sugar into caramel or to color food with caramel.

caraway
The seed of an herb used mainly to flavor rye bread, potatoes, and cabbage as well as some cheeses and confections. It may also be used sparingly in soups and stews.

carbonara
A sauce for pasta made up mainly of eggs, bacon, and cheese.

carbonated water See *club soda*

cardamon, cardamom, cardamum
An aromatic spice contained in curry and used to flavor certain pastries.

carob
A chocolate flavored powder milled from the pod of the carob tree. Also known as St. John's bread.

carotene
A substance readily converted to vitamin A in the body; plentiful in a number of vegetables including carrots, asparagus, pumpkin, and sweet potato, and in fruits such as apricots and oranges. Research has shown that carotene is a significant cancer inhibitor.

carpaccio
An appetizer of thin-sliced raw beef served with a sauce of blended vinegar, oil, mustard, garlic, onion, parsley, and cornichons.

carrot

A common root vegetable served raw or cooked as a side dish or garnish. In spite of their high sugar content, carrots tend to a bitter aftertaste when cooked; for those who find it objectionable, we recommend glazed carrots:

Basic Glazed Carrots (Carottes à la Vichy)
Place sliced carrots in a pot barely covered with water; add butter, salt, and pepper to taste. Simmer gently, covered, until the liquid is reduced; toss the carrots in the concentrated glaze and serve.

Variations on Glazed Carrots:
- Slice carrots thin and reduce the amount of cooking water. Simmer until the water is gone, then allow the carrots to brown lightly in the remaining butter.
- The dish may be enhanced by cooking in orange or other fruit liqueur or juice.

carving
The art of cutting meat, poultry, or game for serving.

In this day of bringing disjointed or sliced meat to the table, the carving of a Thanksgiving or Christmas bird by the head of the household is the only vestige of a day when carving was truly an art, usually performed only by a nobleman appointed to the task.

casaba
A smooth-skinned winter melon with a light skin and white flesh.

cassava
A tropical plant with a starchy edible root that yields tapioca.

cashew
A tropical tree or its yellow-white, kidney-shaped nut.

casing
A membrane used to enclose processed meat such as sausage.

casserole
- A true casserole is a rounded dish of metal or earthenware with a tight-fitting lid, or the food that has been cooked in such a dish. The food to be cooked is placed in the dish and slowly baked; condensation of moisture from the broth and the food collects on the lid and keeps the preparation moist and succulent.
- In general parlance, *casserole* has come to describe any combination of foods that comprise a one-dish meal.

cassis See *crème de cassis*

cassoulet
A delicious casserole of beans, meat and fowl, baked slowly in a tightly-lidded casserole dish.

cast iron See *cookware*

catsup See *ketchup*

cauliflower
A plant of the cabbage family with tightly concentrated white flower stalks that mass together to form a head.

The florets may be served cooked or raw in a salad; steamed and served with butter; or steamed with a variety of vegetables such as tomatoes or peppers, a bit of Parmesan cheese, and spices. Cauliflower, a good source of vitamin C and fiber, is considered a cancer preventive.

Tip: For a dramatic presentation, serve a whole steamed head of cauliflower in a bowl covered with a cheddar cheese sauce to which bits of pimiento have been added.

caviar
The roe of fish, served mainly as an hors d'oeuvre.

The quality of caviar varies greatly, depending largely on the place and type of fish from which it comes. The best caviar is from sturgeon and may cost up to fifty dollars an ounce!

cayenne
A type of pepper, finely ground to a red powder and used as a seasoning. Although cayenne pepper is very hot, it is often added in minute quantities to sauces or soups to bring out their flavor.

celeriac
A type of celery cultivated for its subtly flavored root.

celery
A vegetable with long greenish leaf stalks that usually are eaten raw in salad, or cooked in soup or stew.

Celery leaves, often discarded, are a fine addition to salad, soup or stew as well; dried and crushed, they can be used as an herb for seasoning.

celery cabbage
A mild-flavored varietal cabbage with a distinct celery-like flavor; a tasty addition to salad or cole slaw.

celery salt
A commercial seasoning of dried celery and salt. Unfortunately, the mixture generally proves to be just an expensive way to buy salt: better to buy dry celery and mix your own.

ceramic See *cookware*

Chablis
Originally, a white burgundy wine made in the area of Chablis, France. The term is often used to describe any dry white fruity wine similar to Chablis (and many that are not).

chafing dish
An ornate serving dish with a candle, alcohol burner, or canned fuel receptacle at the bottom to heat food held in the dish. The chafing dish is used mainly for buffet service.

Champagne
* The province of France where the regal sparkling wine of the same name is produced.
* Often used to denote any wine produced by techniques similar to those of the vintners of Champagne.

Tip: Although the sherbet glass pictured on the right is the one we usually associate with a festive serving of champagne, the *flute* shown on the left is the preferred glass as it does a better job of containing the effervescence of the beverage.

champignon
Any of the varieties of edible mushrooms. *Au champignon* designates a dish cooked with or containing mushrooms.

charcoal
A product created by the incomplete combustion of organic matter. Granulated or powdered, charcoal has the ability to readily absorb colors and odors so that, in addition to cooking food on the grill, it is used to purify and clarify liqueurs, wines, and water.

chard
A kind of beet with large edible leaves and stems; also called Swiss chard.

Chardonnay
A type of grape used in the making of white wine such as Chablis.

charlotte
A molded dessert lined with ladyfingers or other cake and filled with cream, custard, fruit, jam, ice cream, or sherbet. The classic, *Charlotte Russe*, is filled with Bavarian cream.

One prepared and chilled, the charlotte is inverted on a serving platter and often garnished further before serving.

charlotte mold
A special pan in which a charlotte is prepared.

As a practical matter, any pan with smooth, sloping sides can be used to form a charlotte.

chateaubriand
A thick fillet of beef garnished with potatoes and other vegetables, served with a Bernaise sauce

Cheddar
A firm cheese named for its place of origin in England.

Excellent cheddar-style cheeses are made in the U.S. and readily available ranging in color from yellow–white to deep orange, and in flavor from mild to very sharp. Although mass–produced cheddar may be satisfactory, the flavor is in no way comparable to that of a quality cheese.

cheese
A product made from curds of soured milk that have been drained, pressed and, usually, allowed to ferment or ripen. Each of the elements that go into the making of cheese has an effect on the outcome, including the milk or cream used, the curdling process, the molding, and the cultures used in fermentation, thus accounting for the wide variety of cheeses available.

cheesecake

A very rich dessert more akin to a pie than a cake, usually having a bottom crust of crumbs and a filling based on cottage or ricotta cheese, eggs and sugar, often with other flavorings added.

cheesecloth

A thin cotton cloth with an open weave, used to wrap certain cheeses for curing.

In the kitchen, layered cheesecloth may be used to wrap a *bouquet garni,* to hold a fish when poaching for easy removal from the pan, or to line a colander or funnel for very fine straining.

cheese cutter

The best cutter for nearly all cheese is the one most readily available on the market: a piece of wire stretched between two prongs. There are more sophisticated devices of wire attached to a board and even some with adjustable gauges that allow one to set the thickness of the slices. Incidentally, most of these devices work equally well for slicing hard boiled eggs.

A cutter more suitable for hard cheeses is an implement that looks like a cake server with a cutting slot built into it. (On a tip from a friend, we also found this one to be an excellent vegetable peeler.)

chef's salad

A large green salad with tomato, cucumbers, onion slices, hard-boiled egg wedges, etc., topped with julienne slices of cheese, ham, and turkey.

cherry

Any of a type of small fleshy fruit with a smooth pit, and ranging in color from yellow to deep red. Cherries are eaten raw, incorporated into a number of desserts, or cooked into certain savory dishes.

cherry pepper

A small round pepper resembling an oversized cherry that may be hot or sweet.

cherry pitter or cherry stoner

A device for removing the pits from cherries. The simplest involves a rod or plunger that pushes out the pit from a cherry (or olive) placed in a small cup-like holder. More elaborate devices feed the fruit from a hopper and have individual channels for directing the cherry or olive and the pit into separate containers.

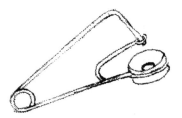

cherry tomato

A small, round, meaty tomato that approximates a very large cherry.

Cherry tomatoes may be served as part of a salad or to garnish a plate. As an appetizer or garnish they are excellent stuffed with bleu cheese, crabmeat, shrimp paste, or tuna.

chervil

An herb whose curly leaves resemble those of the carrot to which it is related. Chervil is used to flavor mild dishes of chicken, veal, or omelets, or to simply decorate a plate.

chestnut

A sweet, smooth-shelled nut of the beech family. Chestnuts may be used as a garnish or as a compote after boiling them in vanilla flavored syrup, but they most usually find their way into confections as a flavoring paste.

chicken

A common term that refers to any hen or rooster regardless of age or type, from a young broiler to an old stewing hen.

In recent years, chicken has gained a reputation both as a healthy meat low in fat and as a risky one that can house harmful bacteria. Fortunately, the risk of contamination can be eliminated through proper storage and handling. Any fowl should be kept tightly wrapped and refrigerated until ready to cook. Above all, after preparing raw chicken for cooking, wash all utensils, surfaces, etc. thoroughly before handling other food.

With flavor strong enough to hold its own against other ingredients, yet mild enough not to overpower, chicken is an ideal component of combination or one-dish meals. It blends well with most sauces, vegetables, and even fruit. Once cooked, it is delicious hot or cold.

See also *broiler, capon, Cornish hen, fowl, fryer.*

Chicken Cacciatore

Chicken simmered with tomato sauce, mushrooms, wine and spices; customarily served with pasta.

Chicken Divan

A dish of sliced chicken that is topped with broccoli or asparagus and Mornay Sauce, then browned under the broiler.

Chicken Kiev

A calorie-laden dish of chicken breasts that have been stuffed with butter and herbs, then breaded and fried.

Tip: The calorie-conscious may want to opt for variations on the theme that are just as elegant: the use of cheese or vegetables for the stuffing and baking instead of frying.

Chicken Marengo

A chicken stew of tomatoes, pearl onions, mushrooms, and spices. See also, *Marengo.*

Chicken Tetrazzini

A combination of chicken, pasta, and mushrooms in a rich cream sauce.

chickpea

A member of the pea family, chickpeas or garbanzos resemble a yellowish-white hazelnut. Whether in *couscous, hummus,* a salad, or soup, they are a tasty and healthy addition to the diet.

chicory

In the U.S., we generally think of chicory as a coffee additive made from the ground roots of wild chicory. The cultivated variety, ever more available in markets, is known as French or Belgian *endive.*

chiffon

Descriptive of food that has been made light and fluffy by the addition of beaten egg whites, such as *chiffon pie.*

chiffonnade

Greens or herbs cut into fine strips or minced for a garnish or for adding to a dish, such as a soup or sauce.

chili

◉ Any of a number of cultivated hot peppers, fresh or dried.

◉ *Chili con carne*.

chili con carne

Literally *red pepper with meat*.

Originally a spicy beef preparation usually made with tomatoes and often including beans, *chili* in the U.S. has come to designate a spicy concoction of beans with tomato sauce that may contain any kind of meat or no meat at all.

The popularity of chili and its innumerable variations are attested to by the many chili cook-offs held with great fanfare throughout the U.S. and by the proprietary names of various concoctions, such as *Texas chili* or *Cincinnati chili*.

chili pepper See *chili*

chili powder

A combination of ground hot peppers used as seasoning.

chili sauce

A condiment of tomatoes, onions, peppers, and spices.

Chinese cabbage See *celery cabbage*

chinois

A cone-shaped strainer; also called a China cap because of its resemblance to a hat worn by Chinese coolies.

The mesh in a chinois may vary from coarse to very fine depending on the use for which it is intended. Commonly employed to strain cooking liquids and sauces, or to purée soft vegetables by forcing them through the mesh with a small ladle or *pestle*, the chinois has an advantage over the rounded sieve in that its output tends to flow toward its pointed tip.

chip

In the culinary world, only *chipped ice* retains the original sense of the word which is that of a small piece, irregular in shape. Our *chipped beef* and *potato chips* are cut in uniform thin slices. The problem of definition is further compounded by our translation of the chips in British *fish and chips* as elongated sticks of potato similar to French fries.

A chip is what you make it; it's a piece of something.

chipped beef

Cured beef that has been thinly sliced.

chitterlings, chitlings, chitlins

The small intestine of a pig, served boiled or fried.

Regarded as a mainstay of country cooking in some parts of the country and disdained in others, chitterlings attain a certain nobility as an ingredient in Andouille, that wonderful smoked sausage of Cajun cuisine.

chive

An herb with long, slender leaves and an onion-like flavor used to season soups, sauces, salads and the like.

chocolate

Flavoring extracted from roasted cacao seeds.

The extraction is available either as *cocoa* or bitter chocolate used in cooking; the addition of such things as vanilla and milk go into making various other types from semisweet to milk chocolate.

Federal law protects the consumer to some extent by decreeing the amount of pure chocolate that must be in a preparation so-named, but inferior brands may substitute other fat for the cocoa butter with an adverse effect on flavor, texture, and keeping qualities, so read the label. Further deterioration of chocolate content and flavor occurs from additional processing and additives that make the concoction 'instant', or at least easier to dissolve, as in ready-made cake mixes.

choke

The hair-like growth in the center of an *artichoke*.

chop suey

Along with *chow mein*, a Chinese-style dish created to suit American taste. Both are a combination of vegetables and meat cooked together in a soy-based sauce. Chop suey is served over rice; chow mein over fried noodles.

chorizo

A spicy, dry Spanish sausage used extensively as a flavoring agent in soups and stews, and as an appetizer.

chow chow

Variously described as vegetables pickled in a mustard sauce or a Chinese fruit preserve spiced with ginger.

chowder

A thick soup to which milk or cream is often added.

chow mein See *chop suey*

chutney

A spicy condiment made with fruit, brown sugar, and vinegar, a traditional accompaniment to curry dishes.

cider

* Historically, a drink created from the fermentation of juice pressed from fruit in much the same manner as wine, though usually with a lower alcohol content.
* In the U.S., most beverages labeled as cider are simply pasteurized apple juice, although true *sweet*, or unfermented cider can be found occasionally.

The fermented beverage may be called *hard* or *still* cider.

cinnamon

A brown spice derived from the inner bark of the cinnamon tree.

citric acid

An organic compound found in a large number of fruits such as lemons, oranges, and raspberries; used in the making of flavorings.

citron

A type of large lemon cultivated in the Mediterranean; used mainly in the making of confections.

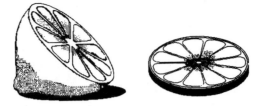

citrus
Designating of lemons, limes, oranges, and similar fruit or the plants that bear them.

clabber
Milk that has soured to form a thick curd.
Pasteurized milk will not sour, but only spoil, therefore, most recipes that once called for sour milk now often specify buttermilk as a substitute.

clam
Any of a variety of hard-shelled bivalve mollusks, eaten raw or cooked in sauces, soups, fritters, etc.

claret
A dry red wine.

clarify
The process of removing impurities or sediment so as to make a liquid absolutely clear. The procedure varies according to the type of liquid that is to be clarified.

clarified butter
To clarify butter, melt completely over low heat and skim off any solids that come to the surface. When the butter is very hot, remove from heat and allow the milk solids to sink to the bottom, a matter of minutes; then draw off the butter fat from the top and refrigerate in a tightly closed container. In addition to its popularity as a dipping sauce for lobster or crab, this butter fat, also called *ghee*, has a high smoking temperature and is therefore desirable for making omelets or sautéing at high heat.

Tip: After clarifying butter, use the milk solids that remain to flavor vegetables or sauces.

Another Tip: When frying, butter and oil in equal portions is a reasonable substitute for clarified butter.

clarified stock

Seldom do we require a stock this clear, but it does make a sparkling aspic and because the process seems almost miraculous, every aspiring gourmet should try it at least once! For each quart of <u>cooled</u> stock, stir in the white and shell of one egg. Heat the stock slowly to a simmer without stirring. Gently push aside the foam that comes to the top just to see that the broth doesn't boil. Simmer lightly for about ten minutes, remove carefully from the heat and allow to rest for about thirty minutes. Again push the foam aside and ladle the broth, straining it through several layers of cheese cloth. The resulting stock will keep well frozen.

filtration

Most liquids such as deep-fry fat or fruit juices can be clarified by filtering through a fine-meshed chinois or sieve, or through several layers of cheese cloth placed in a colander or funnel.

Tip: Be patient when filtering liquids; don't try to press them through a mesh, but allow to flow through naturally.

clay See *cookware*

clove

⊛ A pungent aromatic spice, the dried flower of a tropical evergreen tree (whole clove) that is also available ground.

⊛ A segment, as a *clove of garlic.*

club sandwich

A sandwich of two or more layers with toasted bread between each layer.

club soda

An effervescent water charged with carbon dioxide gas.

Tip: To glean the kids off sugary soda, make fresh fruit soda by mixing equal parts of club soda and fresh fruit juice, or vary the quantity to suit your taste.

cobbler
A deep-dish fruit pie that has as its crust a rich biscuit dough baked either on the top or on the bottom. A cobbler is customarily served with cream, hard sauce, or ice cream.

Cocido
A Spanish soup of chicken, beef, or both, and vegetables that has as its signature ingredients chorizos or other spicy sausage and garbanzo beans.

Cock–a–Leekie
A Scottish soup of chicken and leeks.

cockle
A marine bivalve with a shell similar to that of a scallop; cockles may be eaten raw or steamed.

cocktail
An appetizer of food or drink served at the beginning of a meal.

cocoa
An extract of the cacao bean that is powdered after some of the cocoa butter has been removed

cocoa butter
A fat derived from the cacao bean.

coconut
The fruit of the coconut palm or its edible meat.

coconut milk, coconut cream
- The sweet milky fluid contained naturally in the coconut
- A liquid made by straining a blend of chopped coconut and water. *Coconut cream* is made by blending milk with chopped coconut instead of water.

coconut oil
Oil extracted from coconut meat.

cod
A food fish of the northern seas.

coffee

A dark brown beverage made from the roasted beans of a tropical plant. The characteristics of a particular cup of coffee may be attributed to the origin of the beans, how they are roasted, how they are ground, and the method of brewing. Most coffees are blends, so that, like wine, they are best selected by the brand that offers the desired quality and consistency. Longer roasting produces a stronger flavor, with Viennese and French roast among the darkest. Fine grinding releases more of the essence from the bean, but may also accentuate any bitterness. Brewing methods range from passing hot water or steam through ground coffee beans to simply boiling water and coffee together in a pan. Additions to coffee are also many and varied, from milk or cream and sugar to lemon zest to flavorings added to the beans or to the final cup of brewed coffee. See also *espresso*.

coffeecake

A sweet bread, usually topped with fruit or icing, presumably so-named as it is expected to be taken with coffee.

cognac

A distinctive **brandy** produced in the *Cognac* district in France. Only brandy from this area should be called *cognac*.

cola

An African tree that produces seeds high in caffeine from which are extracted a flavoring agent.

colander

A bowl-like device with handles, perforated throughout with holes large enough to release liquid while holding back all but the finest bits of food. Used to drain the water from foods such as cooked pasta, a colander should not be relied on for washing foods like spinach where immersion is preferable.

cold cuts
A selection of cold, sliced, meat and cheeses.

cole slaw, coleslaw
Traditionally, a salad of shredded cabbage with dressing.
Variations to traditional cole slaw include the addition of shredded carrots, apples, pineapple, green pepper, or onion.

collard
A green leafy vegetable akin to kale usually served cooked with a bit of ham, bacon or salt pork for seasoning.

collop
A small slice of meat or a patty of any food.

comfrey
An English language dictionary describes comfrey as a plant sometimes used for forage or ornamentation, whereas a French cookbook describes it as edible in salad or cooked like spinach. As for us, we just consider it a healing herb taken as a tea.

comino See *cumin*

compote
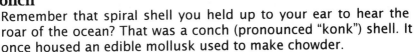

❀ A preparation of fruit cooked in syrup.
❀ A stemmed serving dish.

conch
Remember that spiral shell you held up to your ear to hear the roar of the ocean? That was a conch (pronounced "konk") shell. It once housed an edible mollusk used to make chowder.

condensed milk
A thick milk made by removing part of the water from fresh milk and adding sugar; used primarily in the making of confections. Not to be confused with *evaporated milk*.

condiment
Any seasoning or relish served to flavor food at the table.

confection
Any sweet preparation, usually served at the end of a meal, such as candy, ice cream, or cake.

confectioners' sugar
Sugar that has been ground extremely fine for use in making confections

congeal
To thicken or coagulate.

conserve
Pronounced with the accent on the first syllable, it denotes a kind of fruit preserve or marmalade.

consommé
A clear stock that has been concentrated and clarified.

cook
To prepare food for eating, as by cutting, combining, blending, or exposing to heat.

cooker
❀ An appliance or utensil for heating food
❀ A vessel for holding food to be heated.

cookery, cooking
Specifically, refers to the application of heat to alter the taste and texture of food. Generally, the term is applied to any process involving food preparation

cookie
Any small, sweet confection that is baked.

cookie-cutter
A thin metal form for cutting cookie dough into various shapes.

Tip: For interesting canapés, spread toppings over forms cut from bread with a cookie-cutter. For garnish, use very small shapes to cut decorations from vegetables or gelatin.

cookie sheet
A rigid baking sheet, often with low sides, used for the baking of cookies, other pastries, or breads, and often as a support or drip-pan for other containers in the oven.

cooking oil
Any oil considered suitable for frying by virtue of its flavor (or lack of it) and of its high smoking point. Nut oils, for example, tend to break down under high heat. Olive oil, preferred for most uses, may not be suitable for some frying because of its flavor.

cookware

One of the key elements to preparing food well is having the proper utensils for cooking. To do so does not require purchasing every new gadget, utensil, and special cooker that comes on the market. Most of us ultimately opt for an eclectic selection of skillets, pots, and pans that suits most of our needs.

When buying cookware, consider the critical elements of **size, intended use**, and **composition** or the material of which the utensil is made. Size will depend largely on the amount of food normally cooked at one time: an oversized pan wastes heat and may boil off liquids too rapidly, while crowding food into one that is too small may make stirring difficult. A double boiler is a must for foods that cannot be exposed to direct heat and the elements can be separated to make two sauce pans, but if you don't often need a double boiler, consider a metal mixing bowl that will fit over the top of a saucepan. Selecting material entails a number of considerations:

- **Aluminum** pans, the least expensive available, are worth just what you pay for them and not a penny more! A heavy aluminum pan, however, conducts heat well and is worth the additional cost although it will discolor certain foods and become discolored by others.

- **Cast iron**, which retains heat well, is especially desirable for skillets, griddles, and Dutch ovens; anywhere one desires an even heat. A cast iron utensil should be *seasoned* before using and cleaned by wiping to preserve the cure.

- **Ceramic** cookware includes earthenware, stoneware, porcelain, etc. All are fragile in that they do not take kindly to sudden changes in temperature. They are used mostly for baking casseroles and the like. Follow the manufacturer's directions carefully and look for a guarantee that the pot is lead-free; some unglazed and soft-glazed pots have been shown to harbor toxic amounts of lead.
- **Copper** can be toxic if it comes in contact with certain foods, therefore most copper pots are coated with another metal, often stainless steel (see below). Copper heats quickly and, if thick enough, holds heat well. Copper bowls are often used for mixing egg whites, as the chemical reaction between copper and egg hastens the process and tightens the whites.
- **Glass** is a poor conductor of heat and, unless *flameproof* as distinguished from *heat-resistant*, should not be placed directly on a heat source. Even flameproof pans develop hot spots, however, and we can't think of any reason to use them on the stovetop except to watch your dinner as it scorches. Glass is mostly used for baking at moderate temperatures.

- **Non-stick** surfaces are the space-age contribution to both easy cleanup and health, reducing or eliminating the need for cooking oil. As with any cooking vessel, they should be heavy enough to hold and disperse heat well. In addition, the quality of the finish is important and the use of soft utensils is recommended so that the surface material does not show up as a part of the dish being cooked.
- **Plastic** is not recommended for cooking at all. The surfaces of most plastics tend to retain grease and even in a microwave, the heat of cooked food can dissolve the material.
- **Stainless steel** is second only to non-stick surfaces for ease in cleaning, but it does not conduct heat well; therefore, it is often sandwiched with a layer of aluminum or copper

Note that a reference to poor conductivity simply means that the material will pass heat through to the food it contains mainly at the point of contact with the heat source, thus developing hot spots and cooking unevenly. This is most likely to create a problem on an electric stove where the heating element does not cover the entire surface of the pan and is generally a matter of indifference in baking where the container is surrounded by heat.

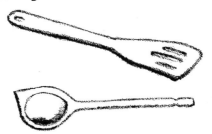

Tip: Seldom do we handle food so hot that metal utensils are required. Although only non-stick pans normally recommend using nylon or wooden kitchen tools, any finish can be scratched and will benefit by having its useful life extended through their use.

copper see *cookware*

coq au vin
A classic dish of chicken that has been browned and fired with brandy, then cooked in red wine with mushrooms and onions.

coquille
Small dishes made in the form of a scallop shell or the scallop shell itself, used to serve a variety of appetizers.

Coquille St. Jacque
An appetizer of scallops and Mornay sauce browned under a broiler and served in a *coquille*.

coquina
A tiny saltwater clam. Only one who visits the seashore is likely to taste the delicate broth made from these diminutive morsels.

cordial
Any liqueur.

cordon bleu
Slices of meat, usually chicken or veal, stuffed with ham and cheese, breaded and lightly fried.

corer See *apple corer*

coriander
A spicy herb of the family that includes parsley and cilantro, used in flavoring apple pie, gingerbread, chili, curry, and sausage. Most of us probably recall the taste best from the flavor of the lowly hot dog.

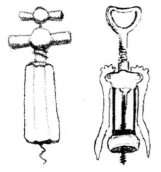

corkscrew
A device for removing a cork stopper from a bottle.

Such devices range from simple corkscrews, many more suited to decoration than to use; the "waiter's friend" used by professionals that is equipped with a hinged section to provide leverage against the rim of the bottle (see illustration at *bottle opener)*; combination openers that allow screwing into the cork and then removing it by turning a second screw or raising a pair of handles; and those that force the cork out with air pumped through a needle inserted into the cork.

corn

To this day in England all grains are called *corn*. In America, the term denotes any of the varieties of native *maize* or *Indian corn* with yellow kernels growing on cobs enclosed by husks, unless it is in a combined word such as *barleycorn*.

corn bread

A quick bread made from **cornmeal**.

corned

Preserved in brine, as ***corned beef.***

corned beef

A beef brisket that has been cured in a solution of salt water and spices for several weeks.

cornichon

A sour pickle; a small cucumber that has been preserved in vinegar. Dill pickle may be substituted when *cornichons* are not readily available, but there will be some difference in flavor.

Cornish hen

A breed of chicken, British in origin. Most common in the U.S. are **Rock Cornish hens**, a hybrid of Cornish hen and Plymouth Rocks.

cornmeal

A meal ground from dried corn. *Stone-ground* is the better tasting and an indication that the germ has not been removed.

Corn meal may be milled to varying degrees of fineness depending on how it is to be used: as the main ingredient in corn bread or corn muffins, as a substitute for flour, or as a coating. Some cooks use both fine- and coarse-ground cornmeal for coating fried chicken or fish; the combination creates a tight batter that causes the food to steam in the resulting shell.

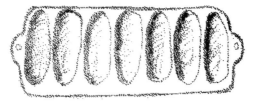

corn pone
Corn bread baked in small oval sticks.

cornstarch
A starch derived from corn, used as a thickener.

Tip: Cornstarch will cook into lumps if added directly to hot liquid, so it must be first dissolved into a cold liquid. Be sure to follow recipe directions carefully, as it will also lose its thickening properties if overheated or if too much cornstarch is used.

corn syrup
A sweet syrup made from cornstarch.

cottage cheese
Any of a variety of soft cheeses made from soured skim or whole milk, then often recombined with milk or cream.

cottage pie
A savory pie of beef, lamb, chicken, or vegetables baked with a covering of mashed potatoes.

court bouillon
A delicate liquid seasoned with vegetables, herbs, and, sometimes, meat or fish; used as a liquid for poaching vegetables or fish.

couscous
Any of a number of traditional North African dishes made with *millet* or *rice* and that may contain vegetables and meat.

crab
To describe a crab as a crustacean with a flat shell, four pairs of legs and two pincers is akin to describing the grand canyon as a big hole in the ground—both statements are true, but neither does justice to these national treasures.

The more common types are *blue crab* found in Atlantic waters, *dungeness* from the west coast, *king crab* from Alaska and *stone crab* from Florida. King crab is valued mainly for its leg meat and stone crab for the claw. Because of the threat of extinction, fishers of stone crab are allowed only to remove one claw before returning the crab to the sea where it will hopefully grow a new one.

Soft-shelled crab is a delicacy highly prized by its devotees. Periodically, throughout its life, the crab grows a new top shell or *carapace* at which time it sheds the old one. The new shell requires time to harden, so that for a few days, the crab is *soft-shelled*.

cracker
A thin crisp wafer often flavored with herbs, cheese, etc.

crackling
Crisp fried pork rind or the browned remains from rendering solid fats, used to flavor other dishes, especially greens.

cranberry
A small sour berry that ranges in color from pink to deep red.
Cranberries are not pleasant tasting in the raw state; however, once cooked and sweetened they make a delightful garnish, condiment, or juice.

crawdad, crawfish, crayfish
A small freshwater crustacean resembling a tiny lobster.
Shelled crayfish may be served with sauce or combined with other foods, but such embellishment constitutes heresy to those who prefer the whole crayfish which is broken apart to 'suck the head and eat the tail'. The only flavoring tolerated for this treat is herbs or spices added to the water in which the crayfish are boiled or steamed.

cream
* The fatty part that rises to the surface of milk and that contains from 18% to 40% butterfat depending on how long the milk is allowed to stand.
* Any food that approximates the consistency of cream.
* Any of various foods that contain cream (*cream soup*) or that are of an extremely smooth consistency (*ice cream*).
* To blend to a very smooth consistency, as to *cream* butter and sugar.

cream cheese
An unripened cheese make from, or fortified with, fresh cream.
For a lower calorie substitute, see *Neufchâtel.*

cream of tartar
A white crystalline powder used in baking soda.

cream puff
A delicate pastry shell filled with whipped cream.

Tip: Cream puff shells are easy to make and provide an excellent container for a light lunch of chicken or tuna salad, or a side dish of creamed vegetables.

cream sauce
A sauce whose main ingredient is milk or cream.

crème de cacao
A chocolate flavored liqueur, brown or clear, that with cream is the base for many traditional cocktails (*banshee, grasshopper, pink squirrel*).
The color of the liqueur has no affect on flavor, only on the coloration of the beverage or sauce to which it is added.

crème de cassis
A liqueur made from black currants, employed primarily as a mixer.

crème de menthe
A mint flavored liqueur, green or clear, used in cocktails or to flavor desserts.
As with crème de cacao, the color has no effect on flavor.

crème de noyea
Noyea is French for *pit*, and this delicate liquor with its almond-like flavor is indeed made from pits, especially those of the apricot or peach.

crème fraîche
A delicate cream made from heavy cream cured with natural ferments.
A credible crème fraîche can be made by mixing without beating, equal parts of sour cream and heavy cream, allowing the mixture to stand tightly covered for about eight hours at room temperature, then in the refrigerator for a day. Note that this will not work with artificial sour cream as it lacks the bacteria required to ferment the mixture.

Crème fraîche is similar to sour cream although better at withstanding high temperatures; it is used sparingly to improve the texture of sauces and purées. *Sparingly* is the operative word here; the small amount required for most preparations means that few calories are added.

Creole, creole

- In French cuisine, a dish served with a garnish of pilaf, or one that includes sautéed peppers and tomatoes.
- In the Americas, a popular style of cooking emanating from the area of Louisiana.

crêpe

A very thin pancake, customarily served with a filling.

As the filling may be sweet or savory, the crêpe is likely to appear as an appetizer, a dessert, or the featured player in a light lunch or brunch.

Crêpes Suzette

A dessert of crêpes folded into quarters to form triangles and topped with a rich orange–butter sauce; usually served flamed.

crockery

Earthenware dishes.

croissant

A rich crescent-shaped pastry often used in place of bread or rolls.

croquette

A small patty or ball of fried meat, seafood or vegetables.

crouton

Small pieces of fried or toasted bread, sometimes flavored with herbs and used to garnish a soup or salad.

cruet
A small glass bottle used to dispense condiments such as oil or vinegar at the table.

cruller
Originally, a rich, doughnut-like pastry made in a long, twisted shape; now often used to describe any doughnut or fried cake.

crumbs
Small bits of bread (see **breadcrumbs**), crackers, or the like incorporated into a dish or employed as a topping.

crumpet
A bread similar to the English muffin, but made with a more liquid batter that produces a lighter product.

cube
To cut into small pieces of uniform size; to dice.

cube steak
A small steak with its surface lightly cut in a crisscross pattern to tenderize it.

cuchifrito
Deep-fried pieces of pork.

cucumber

An elongated vegetable with a green skin, white flesh and a core of seeds. Small cucumbers are often pickled whole; larger, they may be cut up and eaten raw in salad, or pickled.

Tip: To dispel the bitter aftertaste associated with raw cucumbers: spread thin slices in an even layer over paper towels, sprinkle with salt, top with a weight such as a heavy plate, and allow them to rest for about fifteen minutes. Drain and rinse thoroughly before serving.

cucumber pickle salad
Salt, drain, and rinse cucumbers as outlined above. Dry thoroughly with paper towels. Mix with vinegar, a bit of sugar to taste and flavor with herbs—dill is a good choice. Refrigerate

for an hour or two to blend the flavors. Serve alone, in a salad, or as a garnish. These will keep for weeks in the refrigerator.

If a few extra calories are not of concern, drain the vinegar mixture well and toss the cucumber slices in sour cream for a fine garnish or side dish.

Tip: Instead of vinegar, use left-over juice from your favorite pickles.

cuisine
A style of food associated with a particular country, region, etc.

cuisine minceur
French—cuisine of thinness. A style of food preparation developed by Chef Michel Guerard that emphasizes fine food with a minimum of calories and fat.

Cumberland sauce
A sweet mustard-fruit sauce served as an accompaniment to cold meat.

cumin
An herb that is the principle ingredient in curry, and that is also a key seasoning in sauerkraut and many Mexican dishes.

Curaçao
A liqueur made from the peel of a type of bitter orange.

cure
To preserve, as by smoking, salting, or pickling.

currant
A small sour berry that may be black, red or white. The black are used mainly in the making of crème de cassis, the red or white, in the making of jelly and syrups.

curry
A blend of spices that varies according to the locale and the dish into which it is being incorporated.

Commercial **curry powder** is a spice blend that approximates some of the milder curries of India, having among its prime ingredients coriander, cardamom, cumin, allspice, mustard, and cayenne.

custard
A combination of eggs, milk, and other ingredients thickened by cooking over indirect heat or baking.

Custards are generally flavored and sweetened to make dessert puddings, fillings, or sauces; however, it is the same blending of eggs and milk that thickens many baked pasta or vegetable dishes, as well as quiche.

cutlery

These tools of the cook's trade are so important that many chefs carry their own. Not surprising, when you consider how much more difficult it is to prepare food for cooking when the knives are not sharp or are unsuited to the task at hand.

Of the hundreds of styles of blades available, probably the most common, and certainly the most versatile, is the French **chef's knife** with a broad curved blade that can be used with a rocking motion for fine chopping.

A blade of eight to twelve inches is the workhorse of the kitchen, used for carving, trimming, slicing, dicing, and mincing all sorts of foods. A smaller version, with a blade about four inches long, is ideal for paring and cutting decorative shapes.

Tip: If the slicing and dicing that a TV chef does with a few deft strokes looks like magic, it is; and if it looks simple, it is that as well—but it does require some practice. Begin slowly, positioning the food (and your fingers) with care, then slice or mince, gradually picking up the pace as you go. Once comfortable with the moves, you will be amazed at how closely you can emulate the moves of the professional.

Anyone who enjoys **decorating** with fruit or vegetables should have a knife for that purpose, extremely sharp with about a two-inch blade, for cutting fluted mushrooms, radish roses, and the like.

Paring knives, bread knives, and **carving knives** come in a variety of sizes and shapes that one may find useful in addition to the all-purpose chef's knives.

A **boning** or **filleting knife** with a long, thin blade is a must for boning fowl and filleting fish. Although there are knives of slightly different configuration for each job, one good knife can serve both purposes and is a handy blade for other tasks as well.

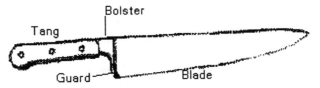

The main parts of a knife are **blade, tang** (the part that fits into the handle), **guard** (a flattening or protrusion at the heel of the blade), and **bolster** (a collar that joins the blade and tang). In the finest quality knives, these are all fashioned from a single piece of steel with the tang extending the full length of the handle.

Tip: When buying knives, consider the **balance** (a chef's knife is easiest to manage if it balances on the blade near the handle); the **grip and guard** (comfortable to hold with a guard to keep your hand from slipping over the blade); and the **bolster**

and tang (a sturdy bolster and a tang that extends the full length of the handle means a more rugged and therefore safer knife). Ideally, the blade, bolster, and tang should be fashioned from a single piece of steel.

cutlet

A slice of meat or a chopped meat patty that is often breaded and fried.

cutting board

A flat surface for holding food that is to be sliced, chopped, minced, etc.

Recent tests have shown that contrary to conventional wisdom, wood boards are more sanitary than plastic ones: plastic boards have been shown to harbor bacteria that tend to die out on a wooden board. Such findings should not, of course, deter one in cleaning the board, especially after using it for raw poultry. The wood surface, incidentally, is also kinder to the blade of a knife.

cuvée

The product of a particular blending of grapes or wine.

dab
⁂ A type of flatfish or *flounder*.
⁂ A small amount.
⁂ To coat lightly, as with flour.

daikon
A large, white root vegetable shaped like a fat carrot that is eaten raw, pickled, or cooked; a Japanese radish.

daiquiri
A cocktail of rum, lime juice and sugar.

dairy
In cookery, cow's milk and products from cow's milk, as cream, butter, and cheese.

Danish, Danish pastry
A rich pastry of flaky dough filled with fruit, nuts, or cheese, often covered with a sugar glaze.

Darjeeling
A tea from India.

date
The nourishing fruit of the date palm.

debone See *bone*

decaffeinate
To remove the caffeine from.

decant, decanter
The process of pouring a liquid from one vessel into another, as wine, to leave behind the sediment. The *decanter*, or container into which the wine is poured, is then used to serve the wine.

deep-fry

To fry by immersing in boiling fat.

The consumption of food cooked in this manner is often accompanied by the sound of arteries slamming shut, but it needn't be so. A deep-frying thermometer to insure that fat is at the proper temperature for each batch of food, using enough fat to cook without crowding so that food is properly sealed, adding food slowly so as to minimize changes in temperature, and careful adherence to cooking times will all insure that food is well cooked without absorbing excess fat.

In addition, some precautions should be taken when deep-frying:

- Use a flat-bottomed, stable pot.
- Don't fill the container more than half full of fat to allow room for expansion and bubbling without boiling over.
- Keep a lid nearby to cover the pan in case of fire.
- Heat the fat slowly to allow evaporation of moisture before it gets very hot and spatters.
- Make sure that food to be fried is at room temperature and dry, also to avoid spattering.

defrost

To thaw or become thawed.

Food from the freezer that is to be cooked or reheated passes through a stage, approximately that of room temperature, which is ideal for the growth of harmful bacteria; the time spent in that temperature range should therefore be minimized:

- Commercial products that caution against defrosting or re-freezing have a purpose: something in the preparation is particularly susceptible to bacterial action, so heed the warning on the label. If such food is defrosted, cook it as quickly as possible—most will still keep for a couple of days if refrigerated immediately after cooking.
- Whenever possible, go directly from the freezer to the stove or oven so that food doesn't linger at a temperature that can cultivate bacteria.
- Chicken, turkey, and ground meat are especially vulnerable. Defrost them in the refrigerator overnight and don't remove them from the cold until ready to cook. To defrost quickly, place in a water-tight wrapping or plastic bag and allow to soak in cold water. (Exposure to the air or to warm water will heat the exterior of the food before the interior is defrosted.)

deglaze

The process of adding a liquid to a pan in order to capture the concentrates that remain after cooking. The method is simple: pour off any excess fat; add water, wine, or other liquid* to the pan; then blend the juices over low heat, taking care to incorporate any bits that cling to the bottom or sides.

*Wine is most commonly used for deglazing. If a recipe calls for bouillon use only the water to deglaze then taste before adding bouillon as you may want to adjust the amount based on the strength of the resulting liquid. It would be a shame to disguise the flavor of a good gravy with cheap, salty bouillon.

Tip: To separate fat before deglazing, pour the juice into a clear, heat-proof container. Refrigerate, and the fat will rise to the top; for quicker results, place the container in a pan of ice water. Skim the fat from the top, or use a bulb baster to siphon the juices from the bottom and return them to the pan.

dehydrate

To remove water. Commercially dehydrated foods such as dried milk, soup, and mixes from which 98% of the water has been removed retain their nutritional value and will remain fresh for years under the proper storage conditions.

delft

A type of earthenware, originated in the Netherlands, usually blue and white.

deli, delicatessen

Literally, delicacies, such as cooked, dried or smoked meat and fish, cheeses, salads, etc. or the place where they are sold.

demi-glace

A rich, brown sauce made from a concentration of brown stock and *Espagñole sauce* with Madeira added.

demijohn

A large bottle, about a gallon capacity, with wide shoulders and a narrow neck, often with handles at the neck and a wicker holder.

demitasse

❀ *French-half cup.* A small cup.
❀ A serving of strong, black coffee at the end of a meal.

desiccate

To preserve food by drying.

dessert
A course of sweets, fruit, or cheese served at the end of a meal. The word derives from Old French "to clear the table", which was indeed the case in the classic French cuisine of the 1800's when a chef's reputation was made at least partly by the elaborately crafted pastries set out at the beginning of the meal to decorate the table. Near the end of the meal, this display was augmented by sweets, and when that course was finished, the table was cleared for a dessert course of fruit and cheese.

deviled
A preparation of chopped food, such as crab, eggs, or ham, seasoned with spices and hot sauce.
The term may have originated as descriptive of food made hot with seasoning, but as most of our "deviled" dishes tend to be relatively mild, we're more inclined to think that they are so good as to be considered sinful.

devil's food cake
There's no mistaking that this rich chocolate cake may be considered by some to be a sinful concoction (see *deviled*).

dice
To cut into small cube. The importance of cutting food to the proper uniform size cannot be overemphasized, not only to make a fine presentation, but for uniform cooking.

Dijon
A city of France known as the origin of a number of gastronomic favorites, such as **gingerbread** and **Beef Bourguignonne**. Probably best known in the U.S. for *Dijon mustard*, a prepared mustard that incorporates white wine.

dill
An aromatic herb that provides both seeds and leaves used for flavoring.

dill seed
The seeds of the dill plant, used primarily to flavor pickles and sauces.

dill weed
The delicate leaves of the dill plant used for garnish and to flavor dips, sauces, fish, and a host of other dishes.

dim sum
A kind of dumpling of Chinese origin comprising dough filled with bits of meat or vegetables and steamed; served as an appetizer or light meal.

distill
To refine by heating that separates the more volatile parts of a liquid, then cooling and condensing to capture the purified substance.

dollop
A small mass or lump of food as *a dollop of sour cream.* An imprecise amount, the size of a dollop depends on the preference of the server.

dolma
A Turkish dish of grape leaves stuffed with meat and rice. Other leaves, such as cabbage, may be used to hold the stuffing, as well as peppers, tomatoes, eggplant, etc.

Dom Pérignon
The monk from an abbey near Epernay famous for the discovery of the process by which champagne is made.

double–acting baking powder
The most common baking powder in use today, its name is descriptive of rising action that takes place both in the cold dough and again when it encounters heat from the oven.

double boiler
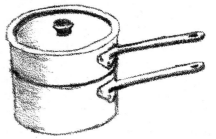
A utensil consisting of a saucepan that fits over another saucepan. The bottom of the double boiler holds hot water which heats food placed in the top so that it does not come in direct contact with a heating element.
Double boilers are used to prepare sauces or confections that should not come in contact with direct heat.
Some double boilers are equipped with a top pan that has a perforated base for steaming foods.

Tip: Use a double boiler to reheat foods when you don't want to stand over them to prevent scorching.

dough
A pasty mass made from flour, liquid and other ingredients, such as for pastry, biscuits, or bread.

doughnut
A pastry comprising a ring of sweet dough that is deep fried and often topped with sugar.

drain
To draw off excess liquid from fresh or cooked food.

drainer See *colander*

dramshop
A tavern or saloon.

draught
☀ Pronounced *draft*, the British (and sometimes American-artsy) spelling for draft.
☀ A drink such as beer drawn from a cask.

dredge
To cover food with a light coating of flour, crumbs, etc.

Tip: Food to be coated for frying or baking must be completely dry to insure an even coating.

dressing
☀ The preparation of food such as fowl for cooking, as by eviscerating, removing feathers, etc.
☀ A stuffing or side dish prepared from combinations of bread crumbs, rice, vegetables, meats, shellfish, or fruit.
☀ A sauce served with a salad or side dish.

dry goods
Although the term generally refers to cloth or related materials, it is often used in the kitchen to describe staples such as sugar or flour.

dry ice
Solid carbon dioxide used as a coolant. Dry ice is so-named because it converts from a solid to a gas without passing through a liquid state.

duck, duckling

Any of a variety of waterfowl that produce dark, sweet meat. Duck is often shunned for its high fat content and its low yield, that is, the high ratio of carcass to meat. We can't contest the facts, but as those who enjoy duck, we manage to work around them nicely:

- First, we always follow the advice of an old recipe that calls for pricking the skin lightly and placing the duck (stuffed only with an apple or onion that will be discarded after cooking) on a rack in a roasting pan, placing it in an oven that has been heated to 450°, then immediately turning the oven down to 350°. As grease gathers in the bottom of the pan, siphon it off and further prick the skin. The result is meat that is not permeated with fat; what is left is a solid layer of fat between the skin and meat that is easily removed.
- As for yield, we satisfy ourselves that the meat is so rich we don't require an outrageous amount, so we serve it accompanied by a couple of side dishes.

Duck à l'Orange, Duck Bigarade

Duckling that has been roasted, braised, or broiled and served with a sauce made from bitter Seville oranges.

dumpling

- ❋ A small ball of dough steamed over liquid.
- ❋ A light crust stuffed with fruit, vegetables, or meat and baked.

Dutch oven

- ❋ A heavy pot for used for braising, baking, etc.
- ❋ A small oven-like enclosure designed for baking on top of the stove or over an open fire.
- ❋ A brick-lined recess in a fireplace that is first heated with hot coals, then used for baking after the coals are removed.

duxelles

A flavoring of chopped mushrooms, shallots, and nutmeg.

earthenware See *cookware*

edam

A mild, semi-soft, commercial cheese traditionally coated with red wax. Copied wherever cheese is made, edam gets its name from its town of origin in Holland.

egg

Of all the foods we eat, eggs are probably the most versatile: served as a first course in aspic or salad; in soups; as a main course in omelets, frittatas, and soufflés; in desserts such as meringue, pudding, or zabaglione; in beverages such as egg nog; and as a thickener or binder for countless preparations.

Some eggs, such as those of the quail, are considered a great delicacy wherever they are consumed. Even the chicken egg, common is the U.S., is a special treat in many other parts of the world where they are not so plentiful.

In the Orient, eggs may be "cooked" by placing them in a pickling solution or burying them in the ground! The chemical reaction of such treatment causes a change of flavor and color that is indeed strange to us. One such results in an egg that when opened releases an aroma which removes any doubt that it should be called "Thousand-Year Egg". Despite its aroma and unappetizing appearance, however, it has a delightful flavor. Such eggs are usually not eaten alone but are employed as garnish.

Most of us prepare eggs by means other than burial and need to keep in mind that they are delicate creatures which turn to rubber when cooked overly long. Whether fried, scrambled, in an omelet, or as a binder in custard, even well-done eggs should be removed from the heat promptly to keep them light and soft.

boiled eggs, hard-boiled eggs, and hard-cooked eggs

Whatever you call eggs cooked in their shells, the controversy rages over whether or not they are more difficult to peel when they are very fresh. We're not about to add fuel to that fire, but keep in mind that unless you live on a farm it is unlikely that you ever have very fresh eggs!

We are willing, however, to offer suggestions for preparing them well. First, puncture the wide end of the shell with a needle, taking care not to go so deep as to pierce the yolk. This allows for the escape of any accumulated gas and permits the white to fill out the shell. As noted above, eggs are best when they are not overcooked. For hard-boiled, place the eggs in a pan with water to cover, bring the water to a boil, remove the pan from the heat, then cover and allow to stand for twelve to fifteen minutes. At the end of that time, plunge the eggs into a bowl of ice water to prevent the build-up of sulfur which creates that nasty green color around the yolk. The result will be an egg that is cooked through with a delicate (not rubbery) white and a bright, clean, golden yolk. Soft boiled requires experimenting with the standing time as it will vary with the type of pan and individual technique.

egg beater

A rotary whisk designed for beating egg whites, cream, and an assortment of other foods.

egg cream

A drink of chocolate syrup, milk, and carbonated water; known in the midwest as a phosphate. Various sources claim that the original New York egg cream actually contained egg or egg white, but nobody seems to know for sure.

eggcup

A small footed container for serving a soft-boiled or coddled egg.

egg foo yung
A Chinese-style omelet cooked with chopped vegetables and sometimes shrimp, topped with a light sauce. A delightful way to dress up leftovers.

eggnog
A beverage of beaten eggs, milk or cream, and sugar, often flavored with brandy or rum.

Commercial eggnog is widely available, but cannot hold a candle to that made from the separated whites and yolks of eggs. The yolks are beaten with sugar until thick and golden, then milk or cream and liquor or other flavorings are gradually blended in. The whites are beaten until they are almost stiff and folded gently into the yolk mixture. Ingredients and proportions depend on individual preference: milk, cream, or a mixture of both may be used; brandy, rum, whiskey, fruit liqueur, or a combination of these may be added. For unspiked (without alcohol), try a bit of orange, pineapple, butterscotch, rum, or other flavoring extract. We always start with at least six eggs and, regardless of other flavorings, add a teaspoon of pure vanilla.

eggplant
A large (two pounds or more), purple skinned fruit that is eaten as a vegetable.

The tender skin of the young fruit is edible, and older fruit may be cooked in the skin to enhance its appearance, such as for stuffed eggplant. Eggplant has an affinity for oil or butter, therefore they should be very hot and used sparingly when frying. Although mild in flavor, eggplant readily accepts the essence of other foods cooked with it and thus lends itself to a variety of treatments.

For two classic eggplant dishes, see *moussaka* and *ratatouille*.

Eggplant Parmigiana
A dish comprised of thick slices of eggplant that have been breaded and fried, sprinkled with Parmesan cheese, topped with Italian tomato sauce and mozzarella cheese, and baked to heat and blend the flavors.

Eggs Benedict
A delightful brunch or supper dish comprised of toasted English muffin halves, each topped with ham, a poached egg, and Hollandaise Sauce, in that order. We used to think that this dish required *Canadian bacon*. After deciding that we preferred thin

slices of sugar-cured ham, we were unable to find any reference to Canadian bacon in our library.

elderberry
A plant of the honeysuckle family or its berries, used in the making of jellies and wines.

emulsify, emulsion
An *emulsion* is a milky liquid that contains minute drops of fat or oil suspended in it. The best example is milk itself which is an emulsion containing minute drops of butterfat.

In cookery, a knowledge of emulsion is of importance to anyone attempting a **Sauce Vinaigrette, Hollandaise Sauce**, or similar preparation.

A Sauce Vinaigrette or French dressing requires a perfect blending of a small amount of oil and vinegar, then a gradual addition of the remaining ingredients. The same is true of Hollandaise Sauce— whether cooked or raw, butter must be added to egg yolks and blended in very small amounts.

enchilada
A Mexican dish of tortillas wrapped around a filling of beef, chicken, or cheese and fried or baked in a sauce.

endive
Any of a number of plants similar to lettuce and having bitter leaves, some of which are served cooked and others raw in salad.

English muffin
A type of yeast roll that is "baked" on a flat griddle and usually split and toasted before serving.

We have not yet found a commercial brand that can emulate the texture and flavor of fresh made English muffins; by far the worst are bargain brands that are dry and crumbly. Good English muffins should be moist and elastic.

enoki
A cultivated mushroom with a tiny head and long stem.

Although used mainly in Oriental cookery, enoki are decorative and can be used in most dishes that call for button mushrooms.

entrée
Although we generally use *entrée* to designate the main course of a meal, its meaning is somewhat ambiguous. From the French it translates as *beginning*, but even in France it does not have that meaning: the entrée may be a single course or several dis-

tinctly different courses that follow the fish (or more properly, the palate cleanser that follows the fish). Go figure.

epicure
One who is well-schooled in and has a taste for fine food and drink.

escargot
A small snail, especially a type that is edible.

escarole
A type of *endive* used primarily in salads.

espresso
A beverage prepared by forcing steam through coffee beans that have been darkly roasted and finely ground.

Grand tradition and ritual often surround the making and taking of espresso and similar coffee beverages, especially in the Middle East where coffee is a vital part of everyday life. Espresso may be drunk with varying amounts of milk or sugar, or a lemon twist, and enhanced with spices such as cinnamon or nutmeg according to local custom.

Tip: Quality espresso has a distinctive flavor, the enjoyment of which, for some, is lessened by the bitterness of the brew. (The espresso purist should read no further, as what we have to impart will only be upsetting—better to skip to the next item and pretend this suggestion doesn't exist.) An excellent brew can be made in a conventional percolator, varying the amount of finely ground, dark roasted coffee to suit ones taste. A pot of ordinary coffee can also be improved by a small amount of dark roasted and finely ground coffee in the bottom of the basket. There—we said it and we're glad!

evaporated milk
A thick milk that has had about half of its liquid removed.
Although evaporated milk may be reconstituted with an equal part of water to substitute for fresh milk, the processing causes a distinctive altering of flavor.

faggot
A bundle of herbs used to season a dish while cooking, tied together for easy removal before serving.

fajita
A course of tortillas accompanied by a variety of fillings such as lettuce, tomato, sour cream, guacamole (see **avocado**), **salsa**, and other condiments with one or more signature fillings of meat or seafood cooked in a special sauce.

falafel
Puréed chickpeas blended with other vegetables and spices, formed into a ball and deep-fried; often served with pita bread.

farce
Stuffing, especially for fowl. See **forcemeat.**

farci
French for *stuffed*. Originally, a cabbage stuffed with sausage or forcemeat, wrapped in cheesecloth and cooked in stock. Now often denotes a stuffed breast of veal that is either cooked in stock or baked.

fast food, fast-food
A preparation served with a combination of condiments and special sauces to create the illusion that it is edible; traditionally served and eaten quickly before the partaker realizes that it is not (edible).

Despite the visions  of cardboard hamburgers and greasy fries conjured up by the term "fast-food", careful selection will reveal that there are some surprisingly palatable offerings available that can even be nutritious, especially if one does not attempt to ingest the food as quickly as it is prepared.

fast food tips

More important, it behooves those who enjoy good food but lack the time to prepare it on a regular basis to adopt some of the fast food techniques to the home kitchen:

- Not all gourmet meals require extensive preparation: accumulate a file of recipes for dishes that can be prepared quickly.
- Make larger batches of soups, sauces, and one-dish meals that refrigerate or freeze well so that they only require reheating for another meal.
- Develop a repertoire of meals that require minimal preparation but relatively long cooking times or that can be cooked on low heat; let a slow cooker do the work while you do other things.

fat

Any of a number of greasy triglycerides found in a solid or semi-solid state in animal tissue and the seeds of plants. They are insoluble in water and melt at a relatively low temperature. Generally, we use *fat* to denote a solid state; *oil* for a liquid.

Other than to suggest that it may be wise to limit one's fat intake, we have no intention of attempting to sort out the various types and their effect on health: first, we're not medicine men and, second, the medicine men are likely to change the 'facts' by the time you read this.

Fat plays an extremely important role in cooking. Despite the trend to avoid animal fat, it is present in all meat, and necessary, for it is responsible for much of the flavor. Fat is needed for the proper browning of certain foods and influences the texture and flavor of others such as gravies, sauces, and salad dressings.

fennel

An edible, aromatic plant of Italian origin with a flavor reminiscent of anise. The stems and bulb are sliced and served raw, often used as a substitute for celery. The leaves are used to season fish or soup, while the seeds are essential to some Italian sausage.

fermentation

A chemical change in food caused by the action of bacteria. Such change may be beneficial as in the production of cheese, wine, or yogurt; it often makes other food inedible.

fettuccine
⊛ Flat narrow strips of pasta.
⊛ Descriptive of a dish made with fettuccine pasta.

Fettuccine Alfredo
Fettuccine pasta tossed with butter, cream, and Parmesan cheese.

fig
The sweet, pulpy fruit of the fig tree. Figs, fresh or dried, are generally eaten raw.

filbert
Also called a *hazelnut*, the edible nut of a hazel tree. Its name derives from St. Philbert's day, around which time the nuts are ready for harvest.

filé
A classic thickener used in Creole cooking, derived from ground sassafras leaves.
Filé is regarded as a possible carcinogen and has been banned for use in foods in the U.S.

filet, fillet
Generally, a choice, boneless piece of meat or fish.
When we mention beef fillet we are commonly referring to *filet mignon*; however, the fillet provides meat for *Chateaubriand* and fillet steaks, as well as the somewhat smaller *tournedos* and *filet mignon*.
A fish fillet is comprised of a single piece of flesh that has been cut away from the backbone and ribs. Most fish will yield two fillets, one from each side; certain flat fish, however, produce two small fillets from each side.

filet mignon
Traditionally, the best of the fillet of beef, taken from the end of the beef fillet or tenderloin.
Modern cutting, in all likelihood, oversteps these bounds as meat cuts tend to vary to satisfy demand. In any event, the *filet mignon* should be lean and tender. There is a tradeoff, however, in that the lack of fat means a lack of moisture and flavor; therefore, filet mignon is generally wrapped in bacon to keep it from drying out during cooking.

fines herbes

A delicate blending of fresh chopped herbs (parsley, tarragon, chervil, or chives) used to flavor a dish that is to be only briefly subjected to heat, such as an omelet.

finger bowl

A small vessel of water used to rinse the fingers at the end of a particular course or meal.

Finger bowls have been perceived as symbols of ostentatious living and the butt of jokes dating back to a time when everyone ate with the fingers and it was common practice to wipe them on the tunic. When use of the fork became more commonplace in the seventeenth and eighteenth century (depending on where one lived) finger bowls became less of a necessity. They seem to be enjoying a minor revival, however, owing largely to the increasing popularity of finger food, especially messy barbecue.

finnan haddie

Smoked haddock, usually associated with Scottish cuisine.

fish

Any of the classes of cold-blooded animals living entirely in water that have a backbone, gills for breathing, and fins. Often we use the term to mean all of the edible animals that live in water.

Because seafood does not remain fresh for long, throughout most of history, few living beyond the reaches of a body of water have been able to dine on the riches it afforded. Modern methods of transportation and preservation, however, have combined to make a wide selection of smoked, canned, or frozen seafood available.

Although any type of processing changes the nature of the food, smoking and canning change it most. While these products may be acceptable, and in some cases desirable, it is freezing that provides almost-fresh (usually sold as "fresh") fish to those who have never seen the sea. Nevertheless, most still lack a knowledge of what constitutes 'fresh'.

To be fresh, a whole fish should have clear eyes that are not sunk back into the sockets, and bright red gills. Whether whole or trimmed, the flesh must be firm and lacking any unpleasant or "fishy" smell. This is just as true of frozen fish as of that which has not been frozen. Any off smell is an indication that the fish was not frozen immediately after it was caught or that it was handled improperly in transport (by being allowed to partly defrost) or was improperly defrosted in the market. Those who are put off by a "fishy" smell have every right to be.

fizz

A tall drink made of lemon or lime, sugar, liquor, and soda water. By volume, the drink is mostly soda water, hence its name.

flagon

A container with a handle and, often, a lid and spout, used either to dispense a beverage or as a drinking vessel.

flambé

Flaming; a dish of meat or sweets to which liquor is added and set afire. The flame not only offers a dramatic presentation, but it cooks off the alcohol and intensifies the flavor.

Our favorite flambé

For dessert, heat in a frying pan, fruit such as blueberries or cherries to which a sprinkling of sugar has been added. When the sugar is dissolved and the berries begin to give off juice, add an ounce or two of brandy, rum, or both and ignite. When the flame subsides, serve over ice cream or rich pound cake.

Tip: For best results, the liquor should be warmed but not boiling. As one never knows exactly what to expect—a conflagration or failure to light at all—we take a conservative approach by starting in the kitchen and, if the flaming is impressive, entering the dining room in triumph to finish serving at tableside.

flameproof

Descriptive of cookware that can be used over direct heat—an important designation, as cookware that is not capable of withstanding direct contact with a heat source can cause serious damage in a kitchen. Best to read carefully the manufacturer's instructions that come with the utensil.

flan

- Generally, in cookery, a type of pie or tart, usually round and lined with a bottom crust. The flan may be filled with fruit, custard, or other sweet mixture to be served as dessert, or with a savory mixture to be served as hors d´oeuvre, brunch, or a light supper.
- In Spanish cookery, a type of custard with a burnt sugar topping.

flapjack

A pancake or griddlecake.

flatbread

A thin cracker-like wafer of Scandinavian origin, made from rye flour.

Florentine

- Designating a dish prepared in the Florentine manner, especially of eggs or fish that are placed on a bed of cooked spinach, topped with Mornay sauce and browned under the broiler.
- Often used to describe any dish prepared with spinach.

flounder

Any of various flatfish, such as turbot, dab, or plaice. Flounder has a delicate flavor and texture; often served stuffed or rolled.

flour

- The finely ground meal of grain, especially wheat. To make grinding easier and improve shelf life, modern flours are usually processed from grain that has had the germ removed. Even so-called "enriched" flours replace only a small portion of the constituents lost with the germ. Wheat germ flour, available in many health food stores may be used in combination with wheat flour to improve its nutritive value.

  Most common on the grocer's shelf are *all-purpose* and *cake flour* although we are increasingly finding *whole wheat flour* and *bread flour* which has a higher proportion of gluten that gives dough an improved ability to expand with the action of yeast. Flours made from rye, corn, rice, chick peas, and soy are also readily available in specialty food stores. All of these lack the gluten necessary for proper rising, however, and must be used in combination with wheat flour for the making of bread.

◉ To coat with flour and (often) seasoning for frying or baking. Food to be floured must be first wiped dry to insure an even coating that will stick to it.

flute

◉ A tall, narrow, footed wine glass used mainly for serving champagne.

◉ A decorative pattern of narrow grooves such as in a pastry mold, or cut into fruit or vegetables.

Fluting is a simple way to dress up a dish for an artistic presentation, either by cutting with a decorating knife (see *cutlery*) or with a *zester*. The knife works best for soft foods such as the

mushroom pictured above, while the zester makes easy work of cutting tougher skin such as that of citrus fruit or cucumbers.

Fruit or vegetables embellished in this manner may be left whole, sliced, or cut into wedges to enhance a presentation.

Tip: Make a colorful border of lemon or orange halves to set off serving dishes of meat, salad, or pastries. The strips of zest cut from the fruit can also be placed around the platter for decoration.

foie gras

French–fatty liver; in cookery, duck or goose liver that has been specially fattened, or preparations made from those livers. In

France this delicacy may be served braised, sautéed, or poached, whereas in the U.S. our primary exposure is to a *pâte* or paste of *foie gras*, not to be confused with a *pâté* or pastry-covered *foie gras*. Got that? If not, see **pâte** and **pâté**.

fold

To blend whipped ingredients gently with a broad spatula so as not to reduce their volume.

fondant

A creamy confection used mainly as icing or a filling for candy.

fondue

- ❉ Descriptive of a number of preparations in French cuisine in which vegetables are reduced to a pulp for later addition to other dishes.
- ❉ Any of several presentations in which bits of food are dipped into a communal pot containing a heated sauce or other liquid. In most cases, a fondue pot, warmer, or chafing dish is necessary to keep the dipping liquid warm.

bagna cauda See listing under *anchovy*

beef fondue or Fondue Bourguignonne

Cubes of raw beef are served to each diner; the beef is skewered and cooked to taste in a pot of peanut oil or clarified butter, then dipped into any of five or six sauces provided. The pot should be a sturdy round one, large enough to accommodate several pieces of meat without lowering the temperature of the oil, and tapered at the top to catch any oil that may spatter.

cheese fondue

A pot of grated cheese that has been melted in white wine and flavored with kirsch into which cubes of bread are dipped.

dessert fondue

Chocolate reigns supreme, but any sweet, thick sauce can be used for dipping bread, cake, or bits of fruit.

shabu shabu

A Japanese presentation that begins with plain hot water* to which a bit of *shoyu* or **soy sauce** may be added, and in which skewered bits of vegetables, seafood, chicken, or very thin slices of beef are cooked. The broth is then served to complete the meal.

*Broth may be used or bouillon added to the water, but it is not necessary as the water will quickly pick up the flavors of the foods that are cooked in it.

food mill

A device used to mill food to varying degrees of fineness.

Like a lightweight saucepan with sloping sides, the base of which is a perforated disk, the food mill is operated by turning a handle at the top which causes food to be forced through the perforations. The perforated disk is one of three that can be exchanged and range in size from very fine to coarse. As complicated as that sounds, the implement is easy to use and extremely efficient for preparing soups and purees.

food processor

Generally, any tool used to slice, shred, mix, blend or in some other way alter the shape or texture of food during preparation. Often the term describes an all-purpose electrical appliance with attachments to do a variety of processing very quickly.

The food processor can be a marvelous convenience and time-saver, especially when preparing large quantities of food that require slicing, mincing, puréeing, etc.

fool

A serving of cooked and puréed fruit to which whipped cream has been added. On occasion we have seen the term used to describe whole fresh fruit such as berries mixed with heavy cream.

forcemeat

Any combination of ingredients that are seasoned and used for stuffing. Forcemeat may be comprised mainly of meat, seafood, fruit, vegetables, cheese, eggs, etc. depending on the dish.

fork

Although reference to the fork dates back to ancient times, they did not come into general use as eating utensils until the seventeenth or eighteenth century.

When forks were first used, they were generally considered an ostentatious affectation—no kidding! Various accountings of the possessions of the royal houses of both England and France in the fourteenth century have revealed the existence of hundreds of spoons and knives, and a mere dozen or so forks, none used for eating. Louis XIV whose dinners were notorious for attention to every detail in the latter part of the seventeenth century is reputed to have shunned forks at the table.

fowl

Any large domestic bird raised for food, as distinguished from *wildfowl*.

freeze

To preserve food by rapid chilling and holding it well below the freezing point. Freezing has become a common means of preserving food and it behooves us to know something about it:

- A freezer should be kept at about 0° to keep food protected.
- Rotation is necessary; even frozen foods deteriorate with time.
- Not all foods freeze well.
- Of those that freeze well, only the best quality will last well.
- Even those that freeze well may need special processing, such as blanching, before freezing.
- Food to be frozen must be wrapped and tightly sealed.
- Frozen from the market is no guarantee of quality—check for signs of improper handling such as **freezer burn** (below) or a damaged container. Cut vegetables should be loose in the package; those frozen into a solid lump are an indication that the package has been allowed to defrost.

freeze-dry

Rapid freezing followed by vacuum drying. Freeze-dried food may be stored for months at room temperature.

freezer burn
A discolored area on frozen food, especially chicken or fish, that indicates improper storage or dehydration.

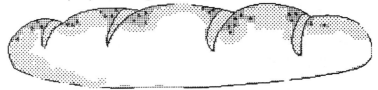

French bread
In France, household bread is a long cylindrical loaf weighing from four to eight pounds with a crisp top crust that is marked with angled slashes. In the U.S., although loaves are usually smaller, some breads purported to be made in the French style are; most are not.

French dressing
Our grocer's shelf sports some red stuff called French dressing that seems to contain a lot of water, sugar, tomato, and a host of chemicals that we can't pronounce and would rather not know about in addition to the requisite oil and vinegar.

Please don't misunderstand—we love the stuff (whatever it is), but if you yearn for the more traditional French dressing, see *Sauce Vinaigrette*.

French toast
Bread dipped in a batter of seasoned milk and eggs, then browned on a hot griddle. Often sprinkled with confectioner's sugar, and served with butter, syrup, and fruit.

Tip: Most recipes tend toward roughly equal parts of egg and milk. Even those who are not concerned about cholesterol may want to try a delicious variation—use about half as much egg as milk, and add vanilla, cinnamon, sugar, and a pinch of salt to the mixture. Buy a loaf of unsliced French- or Italian-style bread and cut it into double-thick slices. By the time the outside is browned, the egg will be cooked through, but the center of the toast remains moist from the milk.

fricassee
Meat, usually poultry, that is cooked in water or stock and served in a sauce made from the cooking liquid. Methods of preparation and seasoning vary according to personal taste. Often vegetables are included, with or without meat, making a kind of stew.

frijoles
Refried beans; cooked beans that are mashed and fried in fat.

frittata
An Italian omelet filled with bits of cooked chicken, ham, or vegetables—often well-seasoned ingredients left over from a previous meal. The filling is mixed with the omelet which is then cooked. A frittata may be cooked in the oven or on the stovetop. When cooked on top of the stove, the top of this thick omelet may be finished off under the broiler, but the traditional method is best: once the bottom is set, a second pan is placed atop the first and they are inverted, allowing the top (that is now the bottom) to cook in the second pan.

fritter
- A griddle-fried cake, often containing fruit or corn.
- A batter containing diced meat, vegetables, or fruit that is dropped by the spoonful into a deep-fryer.
- Pieces of meat, seafood, vegetables, or fruit that are dipped in batter and deep-fried.

fruit
In botany, the mature ovary of a flowering plant; in cookery, only those customarily eaten as dessert. A number of fruits that are not sweet are commonly called vegetables because they are eaten as vegetables. Most of us know that the tomato is technically a fruit; few are aware that the list also includes eggplant, cucumber, pumpkin, beans, peppers, and olives.

fruitcake
A rich spice cake that contains bits of candied fruit and nuts; a traditional Christmas confection.

fry

To cook over high heat in a small quantity of fat or oil. Most frying requires fat such as clarified butter with a high smoking temperature; a reasonable substitute is a combination of equal parts of butter and oil. Food to be seared should be of uniform size, dry, at room temperature, and added to a pan gradually so as to lower the temperature as little as possible. And don't crowd the pan or steam will form and prevent proper browning and sealing.

Tip: Those who prefer to cook without oil should consider each dish on its own merits. Rapid browning to seal in meat juices is best accomplished in the presence of oil that is hotter than a dry pan. In addition, some fats such as butter or olive oil are used to impart flavor to the dish.

frying pan, frypan

A shallow, usually metal, cooking pan used to sauté or sear food. A good pan is a worthwhile investment as it will not only last longer, but make cooking easier. Things to look for:
- Material or a combination of materials that conducts heat evenly so as to avoid hot spots.
- A thick bottom that once warmed requires only a small amount of heat to keep hot.
- A size that fits most needs, depending on the amount of food normally prepared, or a combination of two or three sizes.
- A shape that fits most needs: anyone who frequently cooks omelets will want a pan with sloped sides; such a pan works equally well for most other preparations. Square pans are not recommended as the corners are troublesome when stirring.

- A handle that is sturdy, fits your hand well and, if you are inclined to brown food under the broiler, one that is oven-safe.

Tip: If your frying pan doesn't have a lid, invest a couple of dollars in one of those mesh screens designed to fit over a pan to avoid spatters—it won't replace a tight-fitting lid, but it will hold in enough heat to adequately cover a pan that needs to simmer on the stove for a time.

Another Tip: Non-stick finishes are a great convenience, but for frying they need to be of a quality that will not break down under high heat.

You might want to consider cast iron as an alternative: properly cured, it can be used with little or no fat and is *almost* as easy to clean as a non-stick finish.

funnel

A device like an inverted cone with a hole in the bottom used to direct liquid foods into a container.

A funnel can also be a handy device for straining cooking fat, gravies, etc.: simply line the funnel with several layers of cheese cloth and place over a receptacle.

garlic

Garlic lovers, you have arrived—this pungent bulb made up of sections called *cloves* has come into its own! Throughout the ages numerous claims have been made for the healing powers of garlic. Although not accepted unequivocally, some of those claims, especially for the reduction of cholesterol and for cleansing the blood, have found some credence with the powers that be. Controversy continues, however: we've come across two articles that attest to the benefits of garlic in the diet, one of which claims that garlic should not be eaten raw; the other that it is only effective when eaten raw. As members of the rational fringe, we suggest doing whatever you like. There are, nonetheless, some things you should know:

- Slow cooking in liquid mellows garlic.
- Those who prefer raw garlic can get rid of garlic breath by chewing a bit of parsley. (Now you know why they always put it on your plate in a restaurant.)
- When sautéing garlic, take care not to let it burn as it will turn bitter.

garlic bread

Bread that is spread with garlic butter and reheated.

Here's our favorite recipe, compliments of an old friend: Butter thick slices of French- or Italian-style bread, sprinkle with a bit of olive oil, minced or pressed fresh garlic, and grated Parmesan cheese in that order. Place the bread slices on a cookie sheet and brown them under the broiler. Keep a close watch: they go quickly from nicely browned to overdone.

garnish

- To decorate food, or food that has been decorated to embellish a presentation. See also, *flute*.
- Anything added to a dish to enhance its appearance or flavor. A garnish may be a simple sprig of parsley or a complex preparation such as chutney or a vegetable purée. Many

vegetables that serve as a separate dish at the dinner table are, in a more formal setting, arranged on a platter with the meat or fish course as a garnish. But why wait for a formal occasion? Garnish at every opportunity to enhance the eye-appeal of the food you serve.

garnishes for soup

- A sprinkling of chives, parsley, julienne strips of carrot, seeded cucumber, or scallions.
- Bits of vegetable, meat, chicken, or shrimp.
- Dumplings.
- Tofu.
- Thin slices of orange or lemon.

garnishes for salad

- Fluted cucumbers or radishes. (See *flute.*)
- Chopped tomato bits or cherry tomatoes.
- Julienne strips of carrot, cucumber, or scallions.
- Celery stuffed with cream cheese.
- Anchovies.
- Wedges of hard-boiled egg.
- Bacon bits.
- Dried or marinated black olives.
- Bean sprouts.

garnishes for meat, poultry, and seafood

- Fluted mushrooms, lemons or oranges. (The mushrooms can be cooked with the main dish or served raw.)
- Poached grapes, figs, apple or pear slices.
- Stuffed mushrooms, cherry tomatoes, or small peppers
- Potatoes: mashed and piped decoratively around the serving platter; or small potatoes, boiled or cooked with the entrée.
- A few small shrimp arranged over or around a fish fillet.
- Julienne strips of raw carrots or scallions.
- Any vegetable planned as part of the meal that will add color to the platter, and whose flavor or texture will not be adversely effected by contact with the pan juices.

garnishes for desserts
- Sprigs of mint or parsley.
- Edible flowers.
- Small cookies, cakes, or candied fruit that will complement the dessert.

gazpacho
A Spanish or Mexican soup consisting mainly of cucumber, tomato, onions, and green pepper marinated in seasoned oil and vinegar; served raw and cold.

The liquid in the soup may be reduced and the *gazpacho* served as a salad.

gelatin
A clear, tasteless, odorless substance which in hot water turns to a viscous substance that gels when chilled.

Gelatin is used in binding jellies and other preparations, and to coat certain dishes.

ghee
Clarified butter; see **clarify.**

gherkin
A type of very small cucumber.

Gherkins are used to make **cornichon**, the sour pickle that is a part of many French dressings.

giblets
The parts of a fowl such as the neck, heart, and gizzard that are often used to flavor gravy or soup.

gibson
A martini garnished with a pickled onion.

The story is told of a young advertising executive named Gibson who hoped to improve his knowledge by hanging out with his co-workers after hours, but who had some difficulty in keeping up with his friends' appetite for martinis. He convinced the bartender to serve him watered drinks that could be distinguished from the real thing by an onion garnish. His friends liked the idea, ordered the same, and named the drink after him. Nothing further is known about how his career fared.

gimlet
⊛ A cocktail made from lime juice, sugar and gin.
⊛ A boring tool used to penetrate casks; also used to describe the tool used by a *sommelier* to uncork a wine bottle.

gin
A clear distilled beverage flavored with *juniper* and other congeners known as "botanicals" in the trade.
Gin may contain small quantities of a dozen or more flavorings including citrus, anise, and molasses, but it is the juniper that makes it gin.

ginger
Root stock of the ginger plant used as a spice to flavor many Chinese dishes as well as spice cakes and curry.
Fresh ginger root, far superior than ground, is often available in the market. Slices kept in a mild vinegar or sherry wine and refrigerated will keep for several months. Preserved or candied ginger is also readily available.

ginger ale
A soft drink flavored with ginger.

ginger beer
A beverage similar to ginger ale, but with a stronger flavor imparted by fermentation.

gingerbread
A molasses cake or cookie flavored with ginger.

gingersnap
A crisp molasses cookie flavored with ginger.
Gingersnaps are often used to flavor and thicken gravy, such as for *sauerbraten*.

ginseng
A perennial herb used as a tonic, often taken as a tea.
We were interested to learn that scarce American ginseng is highly prized by the Chinese, while Korean ginseng is believed to be a most effective cure-all for a variety of ailments including

asthma, bronchitis, cancer, diabetes, fever, gout, hangover, and insomnia.

glacé
Having a glossy surface or glazed, as fruit.

glass See *cookware*

glaze
- To coat and bake pottery so as to give it a non-porous surface.
- To coat food with gelatin or syrup to give it a glossy surface. Also, the substance used for coating.

glögg
A Scandinavian drink of heated wine, brandy, spices, and sugar, garnished with raisins and almonds.

gluten
A mixture of proteins present in flour, especially wheat, that gives dough its strength and elasticity.

glutton
One who eats greedily and excessively.

glutinous
Like glue; sticky.

gnocchi
Pronounced *nee-o´kee*. An Italian pasta made traditionally from *semolina*, or from a combination of flour and potato.
The dough or paste for gnocchi is formed into rolls about one inch in diameter, then cut off in one-half inch pieces like little pillows and cooked briefly in boiling water. Gnocchi may be served *al burro* (with butter), with tomato sauce, or with a light butter or cheese sauce. We've also encountered gnocchi made with sweet potato dough—unquestionably our favorite.

goober
A peanut.

Gorgonzola
An Italian cheese similar to bleu or Roquefort, although somewhat harder and milder flavored.

gormandize
To eat like a glutton

gouda
A cheese similar to edam with a somewhat sharper flavor, that also takes its name from the town in Holland where it was first produced.

goulash
Often called Hungarian goulash. A type of beef or veal stew cooked with onions and heavily seasoned with paprika.

gourmand
An ambivalent term that may be synonymous with *gourmet*, or used to describe one extremely fond of good food and drink who is inclined to indulge in them to excess.

gourmet
One who is a good judge of fine food and drink and enjoys both. Formerly in France, an official charged with the tasting of wine.

grade
To classify in terms of quality. Government supervision of grading offers some protection and guidance to the consumer, but the issue is so politically charged that it is questionable how effective that protection is. For example, a number of years ago, when a shortage of *prime* beef (the highest grade) developed, regulations were changed so that more of what would otherwise be graded *choice* (second best) could be labeled *prime* so as not to upset the market. Of course the flip side is that the change meant less marbling in the beef and, very likely, fewer clogged arteries.

graham cracker
A cracker made from a type of whole wheat flour advocated by Sylvester Graham in the mid–1800's.

Grand Marnier
A cognac flavored with bitter orange; a classic liqueur.

granola
A dry cereal mixture of rolled oats, brown sugar, seeds, and various dried fruit and nuts.

granulated sugar
Common table sugar; sugar formed in crystal grains.

grape

A small, round, juicy berry that grows in clusters on a woody vine that is widely cultivated in a number of varieties.

Grapes are eaten raw, dried to make raisins, cooked in a number of preparations, and pressed for juice, most of which is used in the making of wine.

Tip: To complement a heavy meal, top it off with a small dish of yellow seedless grapes that have been carefully dried and mixed with a little sour cream; sprinkle with brown sugar, if desired. The presentation is attractive, and the combination will magically settle the stomach.

grapefruit

A citrus fruit ranging in size from four to six inches in diameter with a light yellow to pink colored rind.

The juicy meat of the grapefruit tends to be somewhat sour largely due to harvesting before they are ripe; however, depending on the variety, they may be very sweet when allowed to mature on the tree. The sharp taste of the flesh and juice adds zest to an otherwise bland fruit salad or cocktail.

grapefruit knife

About the size of a paring knife with a somewhat flexible, curved blade sharpened on both sides, the grapefruit knife is used to cut away the flesh from the rind of a grapefruit half.

grape juice

The juice of the grape, or perhaps, of a variety of grapes.

Commercial grape juice, a distant cousin to the fresh variety, is readily available frozen or in bottles. Specialty stores often carry premium brands that may more closely emulate fresh. Fresh pressed juice of the type used to make fine wine will vary greatly in taste and texture depending on the type of grape, the time of picking, and the technique employed in the pressing.

grape leaf

In cookery, the tender, young, edible leaf of a particular vine that is used to wrap food such as *dolma*.

grappa
A fiery Italian brandy.

grater
Any utensil with a rough surface, usually perforated, that may be used to reduce food to shreds or to particles of varying degrees of fineness.

There are small special-purpose graters such as for nutmeg, flat graters with two or three different cutting sizes on a single surface, and box graters with a different sized cutter on each side. There is also a type of flat grater similar to a *mandolin* with cutting surfaces that can be interchanged; some also have blades that allow them to double as a *mandolin*, though not so efficiently.

Tip: To grate semi-soft cheese, firm it first in the freezing compartment of the refrigerator taking care that it does not freeze and use the coarsest cutting surface or setting.

gratin See *au gratin*

gratiné
Descriptive of a dish served with a browned top crust of cheese or bread crumbs.

gravlax
A Scandinavian dish of salmon marinated in a dill sauce.

gravy
Juices resulting from cooking, usually of meat, or a sauce made from the cooking juices.

Ones definition of gravy depends largely on heritage. For some, only thickened pan juices served with meat and potatoes or rice are called gravy; others consider any sauce, however rich or elegant it may be, a gravy. We still find it strange to hear *Italian tomato sauce* served over pasta referred to as gravy.

grease
Melted animal fat; often used to denote any thick oily substance.

green bean
In common usage, the immature seed pod of a member of the lima bean family, served as a vegetable. Green beans are a good source of both fiber and iron.

greengrocer, greengrocery
A shop that deals mainly in fresh fruit and vegetables.

green onion
An immature onion with long, spear-like leaves, usually served raw in salads or as a garnish for other dishes. See also, *scallion*.

green pepper
Strictly speaking, the immature fruit of any pepper; however, in cookery, green pepper generally designates the mild **bell pepper**, also called *sweet pepper* and in some places, *mango* though no relation to the fruit. Because of their bulbous shape, these peppers, whether green, yellow, or red, are especially suited to stuffing.

Removing the peel from a fresh green pepper seems a most exacting task according to the instructions we've found which call for placing them briefly in an oven or in hot fat, or for scorching them over a flame. The simplest method seems to be that recommended by a popular cooking show host who suggests using a vegetable peeler on the high spots, then cutting them apart in strips and trimming off the rest! Incidentally, all of the seeds and inner membranes should be removed from fresh peppers.

Years ago, we planted sweet peppers and hot peppers side by side not realizing that they would cross-pollinate. The green bell peppers all had a distinctive bite. Husband was delighted; wife who is extremely sensitive to hot peppers was not amused.

greens
Any cultivated or wild leafy vegetable, whether served raw, as for salad, or cooked.

green tea
Tea that has not been fermented before drying; see *tea*.

grenadine
A sweet syrup made from the juice of the pomegranate (*grenade* in French) and used to flavor beverages and desserts.

griddle
A flat cooking surface of heavy metal, usually cast iron. The griddle may be a pan or part of the stove-top.

griddle cake
A pancake; a flat cake made from batter and cooked on a griddle.

grill
* An outdoor cook stove comprised of a heat source, usually, gas or charcoal, with a metal framework for holding the food to be cooked. A *barbecue*.
* An indoor appliance of similar design, with gas or electric as the heat source.

Tip: Do not attempt to cook with charcoal indoors as the burning emits toxic fumes.
* To cook food over an open flame.

grinder
* A large sandwich made up of a variety of ingredients and condiments on a long roll. Also called a hero sandwich or submarine.
* A device for milling food to varying degrees of fineness, as a *coffee grinder*.

grits
A cereal made from coarsely ground *hominy*. Served especially in the southern states as an accompaniment to breakfast eggs or seafood.
Although customarily served with only a little salt and butter to season them, grits are light in flavor and take well to the addition of ham, bacon, or cheese.

grog
Originally an alcoholic beverage, especially rum, diluted with water; a term coined by the British navy.
Today we often use the term to casually denote any liquor, although we have found at least one mention of it as a hot rum drink.

ground beef, ground meat

Beef or other meat that has been chopped or ground to varying degrees of fineness depending on its intended use.

Ground meat is used in a variety of preparations such as **hamburgers**, **meatballs**, and **meat loaf** that may be made entirely from beef or from a combination of beef, veal, lamb, or pork.

Meatballs and meat loaf are best made from meat ground to a finer texture than that customarily used for hamburgers.

Tip: Uncertainty about the quality of ingredients and the poor keeping quality of meat after it is ground are both strong arguments for anyone who frequently cooks with ground meat to obtain a **meat grinder**. Additions to the meat, such as peppers, celery, or onions may be ground with the meat just before cooking as well.

grouper

A food fish that is plentiful along the Atlantic Coast and in the Gulf of Mexico.

The meat of the fish is firm, white, and flavorful. Grouper fillets or steaks may be used in virtually any recipe that calls for fish— delicious with light seasoning, as with butter and lemon, they also thrive in the presence of other ingredients, such as in a bouillabaisse or fish stew.

Gruyère

A rich semi-soft Swiss cheese. A delightful accompaniment to fruit, Gruyère is also well-suited to the making of sauces such as Mornay, or in a cheese fondue.

guacamole See *avocado*

guava

A tropical fruit whose mild-flavored meat is used mainly in the making of jellies or jams.

gumbo

A vegetable soup thickened with *okra*; usually made with tomatoes and chicken or seafood; a traditional Creole dish.

haggis

The national dish of Scotland, made from the heart, liver, and lungs of a sheep, seasoning, oatmeal, and suet that are boiled in the sheep's stomach. The dish is traditionally served with great fanfare, accompanied by an escort of pipers.

halvah

A Turkish confection of ground sesame seeds, nuts, and honey.

ham

A leg of hog that has been salted and smoked.

It is smoking and sometimes aging that gives a particular ham its distinctive taste and character. Ham is popular as an appetizer, as a main dish, or as a flavoring for other dishes.

A few things to remember about ham:

- *Fresh ham* is not ham at all—it is simply pork from the hind quarter that has not been cured.
- **Check the label:** some ham requires cooking and like all pork must be brought to 160° internal temperature to destroy harmful trichinae; unique among canned foods, some canned hams require refrigeration.
- For a special treat, try one the 'classic' hams such as a Virginia *Smithfield*, German *Westphalian* or Italian *prosciutto*. They are expensive, but customarily served in small portions as an appetizer or garnish.

hamburger

Ground beef, or a serving of ground beef on a roll with various vegetables and condiments.

An American variation of *Hamburg steak* which is a mixture of ground beef or veal, bacon, milk-soaked bread, and seasoning. Having come up in a generation rife with jokes about commercial establishments that stretch their meat by adding bread, we will venture an opinion: the addition of moist bread to the meat does indeed make a juicier hamburger. Some other concoctions to consider for the next Sunday barbecue:

- Pack a slice of onion *inside* the burger before cooking.
- Stuff the burger with bleu or cheddar cheese—not too much or it will break through and drip all over the place.
- Mix a little finely chopped celery, onion, or pepper with the meat.
- Use the recipe for your favorite meatloaf and shape it into burgers for cooking on the grill—you'll never be satisfied with plain ground beef again!

hard sauce
A creamy sauce of butter, sugar, and flavoring, sometimes brandy, served over pudding or cake.

hardtack
A hard, unleavened bread or wafer; a one-time staple of army and navy rations.

hare
A mammal similar to the rabbit, though somewhat larger.
The hare more often finds its way to the dinner table in Great Britain or Europe than in America.

haricot
⊛ A well-seasoned stew of mutton with potatoes and turnips.
⊛ Mainly in Britain, a type of kidney bean.

Harvard beets See *beets*

hasenpfeffer
A German stew of rabbit or hare cooked in a vinegar marinade.

hash
Did hash get a bad name because it was traditionally made from leftovers, or leftovers a bad name because they are often made into hash? Either way, the only hash that comes pleasantly to mind is corned-beef hash which at today's prices is unlikely to be a leftover.
There are a number of ways to make hash and with a little creativity any of them can be delightful;

- For improved flavor and eye-appeal, dice the meat or fish rather than mincing or grinding it.
- Bind the hash with a white or brown sauce.

109

- Add bits of diced vegetables such as carrots or scallions for color and flavor.
- Flavor the hash with curry or other spices.
- Top with mashed potatoes and brown off in the oven.
- Serve hash in baked potato shells.

hash browns, hashed browns

Cooked potatoes that have been chopped and browned in a fry pan, often with onion or green pepper added.

haute cuisine

Fine food, often classic dishes, prepared by an able chef.

hazelnut See *filbert*

head cheese

A type of jellied meat sausage prepared from the bits of meat contained in a calf's head.

health food

⊛ Food that is considered to be especially healthful, particularly that grown organically without the use of pesticides.

⊛ Descriptive of foods purported to have special healing or nutritive properties.

hearts of palm

The edible heart of a palm tree; widely used in Oriental cookery.

heat proof

Indicating a utensil, usually glass or plastic, that should not suffer from exposure to direct heat.

Standards differ so that it is best to read the label to be sure exactly what constitutes safe usage.

heavy cream

Whipping cream that contains at least 36% butterfat.

herbs and spices

The difference between herbs and spices? Sorry. We combined them in one entry in order to avoid that question.

The dictionary defines an *herb* as a seed plant that withers completely away after a season's growth, and a *spice* as a vegetable substance used to season food, but that defines an herb as well. Perhaps we can settle the issue with the statement that an *herb* is generally the leaf or stem of a plant, used fresh or dried, while a *spice* is the fruit, seed, nut, bark, or root of a plant, usually dried. Whew!

Despite the wide variety of herbs and spices available to us, unless steeped in cookery, we tend to gravitate to a familiar few. The entries throughout this book give only a hint of the ways in which they can enrich and enliven the foods we eat.

Try some new combinations now and then. There's nothing wrong with an old family recipe, but you never know when a little experimenting will create a new 'old family recipe' that will be passed down to succeeding generations. And if you don't have an herb garden, try some of the fresh herbs that appear in the market from time to time. So what if the family gets tired of having everything flavored with dill for a week or two—just invite the neighbors in and you will all learn something, for fresh herbs impart a bouquet that just cannot be emulated by those that have been dried.

See also *anise, basil, bay leaf, black pepper, caraway, cardamom, cayenne, chervil, chili powder, chives, cinnamon, clove, coriander, cumin, curry, dill, fines herbes, ginger, mace, marjoram, mint, nutmeg, oregano, paprika, parsley, peppercorn, peppermint, rosemary, saffron, sage, tarragon,* and *turmeric.*

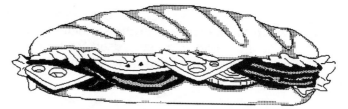

hero
Yet another name for a type of large sandwich of meat, cheese, etc. served on a long roll with lettuce, tomato and a variety of other condiments.

herring
A fine-boned fish that has achieved its greatest popularity when *kippered* or pickled.

We thought we had arrived in herring heaven years ago when we attended what was purported to be a classic Scandinavian smörgårsbord of four courses, each laid out on a large, tiered table. Although herring preparations figured prominently in two courses, a third was comprised entirely of no less that twenty different dishes of pickled herring!

Save the Family ...is the translation of the name for this popular Swedish dish, or so we were told:

In the center of a large tray place a mound of well-drained pickled herring. Encircle the herring with a ring of sour cream. Around the edges of the tray, mound a variety of finely-chopped condiments such as hard-cooked egg yolk, hard-cooked egg whites, cucumber with the skin and seeds removed, pickled beets, parsley, scallions, etc. Serve as an appetizer, a light lunch or supper, or as part of a buffet.

hibachi
Japanese—fire bowl. A small charcoal grill used extensively for cooking in Japan.

Various adaptations have found their way to the U.S. and are often used for barbecuing small quantities of food.

highball
A tall drink made from whiskey and a sweet soda, usually ginger ale.

hoecake
A thin cornmeal bread said to have acquired its name from the practice of placing the batter on a hoe which was held to the fire for baking.

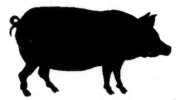

hog
Any swine, usually domesticated, ready for market.

hogshead
A large barrel or cask.

Hollandaise Sauce
A classic sauce made from butter and egg yolks, Hollandaise comes under the heading of 'feared preparations' for it is an **emulsion** and will separate if not properly prepared. There are a number of variations on this sauce, all of which are delicious and outrageously rich.

We have seen recipes for mock Hollandaise that attempt to remove some of the risk and the calories, but they seem to be much more bother to fix and are not nearly as good, without eliminating all that many calories, so we've avoided them, preferring to reduce the amount we use (or at least try to).

Our favorite prescription for Hollandaise is based on one contained in *The Joy of Cooking* that calls for the use of a blender and we can indeed attest that it is deserving of its 'never-fail' reputation. We do prefer hand mixing, however, so it has been modified:

In the top of a double-boiler or metal mixing bowl, whip three egg yolks with a wire whisk, then beat in about two tablespoons of fresh lemon juice or one tablespoon of tarragon vinegar. Place the pan or bowl atop a pan of boiling water, but do not allow it to rest in the water. Continue to beat the yolks while slowly adding one-half cup of melted butter, taking care to completely blend the butter before adding more. When the sauce begins to thicken, add a pinch of cayenne and salt to taste. Continue cooking and stirring until the sauce is the desired thickness; serve immediately. A sauce that breaks down can often be recovered by whipping in a tablespoon of very cold water or heavy cream.

An electric hand mixer may by used, but it's not as effective in scraping clear to the bottom of the bowl as the sauce thickens.

hominy
Dried corn that has had the hull and germ removed.

honey

A thick, sweet syrup processed from the nectar of flowers by bees. Various types of honey take on the flavor of those plants most plentiful in the region where they are produced.

honeydew

A sweet variety of melon with smooth white rind and greenish flesh.

Hopping John

Black-eyed peas cooked with onions, garlic, and salt pork. A traditional New Year's Day dish throughout the South.

hors d'oeuvre

An appetizer of light food served at the beginning of a meal or between courses.

horseradish

 Another member of the cabbage family, cultivated for its pungent root. For the best flavor, buy fresh horseradish root when it is available, peel and grate it, mix with vinegar, and store in the refrigerator. For grating, we recommend a blender; horseradish can be grated by hand, but not without the shedding of tears if it is any good. And if you don't shed any tears, try to get your money back.

⚜ **Horseradish sauce** for boiled beef or game is made by adding horseradish and a bit of dry mustard to *béchamel* sauce.

⚜ **Horseradish dressing** for salad is made by adding horseradish to a *French dressing*.

⚜ **Garnish** for cold hors d'oeuvre may be prepared from a mixture of equal parts horseradish and butter or horseradish and mayonnaise. Chill to allow the flavors to blend.

hot cake

A pancake, perhaps so-called because it is at its best when fresh and hot.

hot dog

A wiener or frankfurter.

Like *hamburger*, *hot dog* often describes the meat enrobed in bun and condiments. Suffering from a bad rep ('hot dog' is said to derive from the idea that they were made from dog meat), hot dogs have been updated. Made entirely from beef, from turkey, made leaner, and even made without meat, they are a popular, and sometimes healthful, food.

hot plate
A small portable appliance with one or two burners, often used for preparing food at tableside.

hummus
A purée of *chickpeas*, *tahini*, lemon, and garlic served as a dip with fresh *pita* bread wedges.

hush puppy
A small ball of cornmeal dough that has been deep-fried.
A traditional accompaniment to seafood throughout the southern states, hush puppies often are prepared with a small slice of pepper or scallion fried inside.

husk
The dry covering of many fruits and seeds such as that of corn which is usually discarded or of wheat which is among the most nutritious parts of the grain.

hutch
A cupboard with an enclosed area or drawers in the base and open shelves for the display of tableware in the top.

hydrate
To combine or recombine with water.

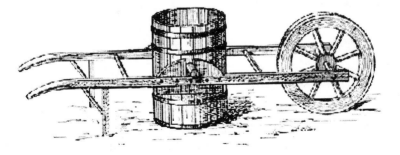

ice

* A frozen dessert such as **sherbert** or **sorbet**.
* Shaved ice served in a cup with flavored sweet syrup poured over; commonly called Italian ice.
* To spread a frosting or other preparation over cake.
* To thoroughly chill a dish, glass, implement, or food.

iceberg lettuce

A variety of lettuce with crisp, green, tightly packed leaves, popular as a salad ingredient.

ice cream

Iced cream and flavored ices in one form or another have a history that is said to date back four thousand years to ancient China.

Purists may disagree, but with so many commercial varieties available, some of excellent quality, it is difficult to justify taking the trouble at home to make ice cream that may not be as good as that which we can purchase.

ice milk

A confection similar to ice cream that contains less butter fat.

icing

A sweet preparation of sugar or honey and other ingredients used to coat pastries and cakes.

Icing may be cooked or uncooked. A simple icing can be easily made by blending three to four cups of confectioners' sugar with one-half cup of butter or margarine and a little vanilla extract. Other extracts, syrup, or fruit can then be added to achieve a desired flavor. A few tablespoons of milk may be required to bring the icing to spreading consistency.

This basic icing, made very stiff and colored, is also quite good for piping decorations onto a cake.

immature

Unripe or not fully grown.

In the world of food, *immature* may as often be descriptive of a plant, cheese, or other food that is just right for consumption as of one that is not yet ready.

immersion heater

An electrical device that heats water or other liquids while submerged in them, often used in commercial kitchen appliances.

infusion

That extracted from steeping in water or other liquid, as of a tea bag in water.

Irish coffee

Coffee to which a small amount of whiskey and sugar has been added, topped with whipped cream.

Whipped cream from a can may be adequate for most uses, but not for this one. The cream should be whipped until it is thick, but not stiff. Float the cream on the coffee by pouring slowly over the back of a spoon, then enjoy the luxury of sipping hot coffee filtered through cold cream.

Irish stew

A lamb stew prepared with potatoes and onion.

iron See *cookware*

Italian bread

A stiff-crusted bread similar to French bread, but generally made in shorter, fatter loaves.

Italian ice See *ice*

Italienne, à la

Indicating a dish prepared in the Italian manner. Hardly definitive, its use depends on the chef's perception of what constitutes Italian style—served with pasta, topped with tomato sauce or Parmesan cheese, etc.

jalapeño
A kind of hot pepper, originally from Mexico.

jam
A preparation of fruit and sugar, boiled down to a thick mixture.

jambalaya
A *jumble* as close as we can figure, but a delicious one.
Variously described as a stew or casserole, jambalaya is a Creole dish of rice, tomato, and onions that may contain other vegetables, meat, seafood, or a combination of all three.

jar
A cylindrical container of glass or earthenware, usually with a top and no handles.

jar opener See *bottle opener*

jasper
A type of matte-surfaced porcelain made by Wedgwood in a distinctive blue or green color with a raised design in white.

jelly
A soft, somewhat transparent food produced naturally by reducing a fruit and sugar mixture, beans, or meat stock, or induced by the addition of *gelatin,* and chilled.
See also *gelatin, jam.*

jellyfish
An aquatic invertebrate, characteristically bell-shaped with long tentacles and gelatinous flesh; mainly used in Oriental cookery.

jellyroll
A thin layer of sponge cake that is spread with jelly or jam and rolled, then sliced to serve.

jerky
Originally, beef cut into thin strips and dried in the sun. Now often applied to other types of meat as well that have been preserved by drying.

jeroboam
A wine bottle with a capacity of a little over three quarts.

Jerusalem artichoke
The edible tuber of a North American sunflower that has a taste somewhat reminiscent of the true artichoke.

Johnnycake
A type of corn bread baked on a griddle; often used to describe any type of corn bread.

juice
* Liquid squeezed from fruit or vegetables.
* The liquid extracted from food, especially meat, during the cooking process.

juicer
Any of a variety of electrical or mechanical devices for extracting juice from fruit or vegetables. The juicer pictured on the left, above, is made from glass and has a slotted ridge designed to contain the seeds while allowing the juice to flow down to the outer rim. The one on the right is a wooden tool that is inserted into the cut fruit and is especially convenient for extracting a small amount of juice when cooking.

julep
The dictionary defines *julep* as a mixture of sugar and water taken with medicine, but we know it as a *mint julep,* a mixture of sugar, bourbon, and crushed mint served over cracked ice.

julienne
* Vegetable or meat cut into thin strips as an ingredient or garnish. Cutting these delicate strips is usually accomplished

by cutting thin slices of uniform length, then piling the slices and cutting across them.

✵ A vegetable soup made from consommé to which thin strips of lightly sautéed vegetables are added.

juniper
The dried berries of an evergreen.

Oil extracted from the berries is used to give gin its singular flavor; the berries are used to season marinades and preparations such as *sauerbraten* or *sauerkraut*.

kale
A member of the cabbage family with curled, spreading leaves that do not form a head, similar to *collards*.

kebab, kebob
A dish of Turkish origin, designating skewered meat, often marinated, and usually cooked over hot coals.

Popular barbecue fare, kebabs are may be made up of chicken, beef, lamb, or seafood, interspersed with vegetables such as green peppers or onions, and fruit such as pineapple or lemon. Incidentally, *shish kebab* is the Turkish name for skewered lamb.

kedgeree
A traditional English breakfast dish of rice, fish, boiled eggs, and cream, adapted from the Indian dish which also contains lentils.

kefir
A beverage of fermented cow's milk.

One source notes that after a day of fermentation, light kefir that is slightly laxative is obtained; after two days, medium kefir that is no longer laxative; and after three days, strong kefir that is slightly constipating.

kelp
An iodine-rich seaweed, often used as a substitute for table salt or taken as a nutritional supplement.

kernel
* A grain or seed encased in a husk, as of corn or wheat.
* The edible inner part of a nut or pit.

ketchup
A thick condiment made from puréed tomatoes, onions, and a variety of spices.

Most people won't be surprised to learn that commercial production of ketchup as we know it began with Henry Heinz over a hundred years ago, but few are aware that *ketchup* is a corruption of the Chinese name for a fish sauce and that until the late nineteenth century it designated any similar puréed condiment.

kettle
* A lidded metal container used for cooking. Generally, in this context, referring to a very large pot with handles on both sides or that may be footed and have a curved handle attached to each side for carrying or hanging.
* A teakettle. A vessel in which water is heated, as distinguished from a *teapot*, in which dried leaves are *steeped*.

kidney
A part of the animal not nearly as welcome at the dinner table in the U.S. as in England where steak and kidney pie or pudding is a tradition.

kidney bean
The large, reddish, edible seed of a common garden bean; shaped like a kidney.

king crab
A large spider crab obtained mainly from Alaskan waters and prized for its delicate leg meat.

kipper
To cure fish, usually herring or salmon, by salting and smoking.
The character of kippers can vary considerably based on the kind of fish used, the way in which they are processed, and whether or not they are canned.
Canned kippers, packed in water or oil, are of a somewhat different texture than those purchased at a deli, but tasty, nonetheless. Served straight from the can, the salty fish is a fine complement to a serving of unsalted scrambled eggs.

kir
An aperitif of chilled white wine with a small amount of *crème de cassis*, a black current liqueur.

kirsch
A cherry brandy from Germany used in flavoring confections and as a traditional ingredient in cheese *fondue*.

kitchen shears
A variety of cutting tools designed for use in the kitchen.
These shears range from light-weight scissors for cutting paper frills, candy wrappers, or pan linings, to heavy-duty implements that can cut through chicken bones.

kiwi
A New Zealand fruit with a brown, hairy rind and sweet, green flesh. In addition to being flavorful, kiwi makes a colorful garnish for salads, cold seafood platters, or dessert.

klatch, klatsch
A casual gathering, as for coffee and conversation. Anyone surprised that *klatsch* is a German word that means *gossip*?

knackwurst
A thick, spicy sausage, cousin to our ubiquitous hot dog.

knead

To mix or 'work' by repeatedly folding over and pressing together, as dough, usually with the hands.
Kneading smoothes dough and develops the gluten that gives it
the elasticity to hold together as it expands when rising.

knife See *cutlery*

knife sharpener

A stone or device for sharpening knives.
The purist will want to use a stone, but the uninitiated should
take care, for it is infinitely easier to dull a knife on a stone than
to sharpen it. It is a skill worth cultivating and that can be a
source of great pleasure, however, especially when friends recognize your talent and ask to have their knives sharpened. Begin
by purchasing a good stone with an equally good set of instructions.
Those with less patience may be better served by one of the patented devices available on the market. Look for one with a fine
stone that will put an edge on the blade without grinding off a
lot of metal and with a firm guide that will aid in positioning the
blade against the stone at the proper angle.

kohlrabi

A member of the cabbage family cultivated for the edible, bulbous portion of its stem.

kosher

⊛ Clean or fit to eat according to Jewish dietary law.
⊛ Descriptive of food prepared in accordance with Jewish dietary law or tradition, such as *kosher dill pickles*.

kreplach

A small dumpling filled with meat, usually served in soup.

kümmel

A liqueur flavored with caraway.

kumquat

With the appearance of a miniature orange, the kumquat has a
sweet rind and sour pulp.
Used mainly in preserves and candies, kumquats also make an
attractive garnish.

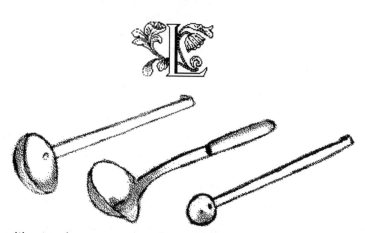

ladle

A cup-like implement with a long handle for skimming or serving. Those used for skimming may have the handle set off at an angle, whereas serving ladles usually have longer handles that rise up straight from the bowl, both to facilitate reaching the very bottom of a deep pan, and to neatly add sauce to a serving of food. Most of the ladles used in a professional kitchen are precise measures as well, such as of two, three, or four ounces. Perforated ladles are used to remove pickles, fruit, etc. from their liquid bath; often made from wood for use in a pickling solution.

ladyfinger

A small oblong sponge cake usually served plain or with fruit or sugar icing sandwiched between two of the cakes. Ladyfingers may be used as well to line dessert molds; see *charlotte*.

lager

A *beer* that is bottom-fermented and typically stored for a period of one to three months to mature. For the most part, lagers are pale in color and light in flavor; most familiar in this country are the relatively bland *pilsner* type brews.

lamb

The meat from young sheep that contrasts markedly with *mutton*, the stronger meat from mature sheep.

lard

- Cooking fat that is melted down from pork fat; used extensively to make biscuits or crusts light and fluffy.
- *Leaf lard* is lard of the best quality, rendered from the leaf fat around the kidneys.
- To moisten and flavor by inserting strips of pork or bacon fat into meat or poultry before cooking; see **larding tool, lardons**.

larder

- The pantry. Any place for storing food; originally a storehouse for bacon.
- The supply of provisions for a household.

larding tool

A utensil in the form of a needle or hollow tube used to insert *lardons* into meat or poultry to moisten and flavor them.

Larding with fat is a practice fast falling out of favor in American kitchens as we become more concerned about the amount of animal fat in our diet and increasingly turn to moist heat for cooking lean meat.

Tip: Use a larding tool to insert thin strips of vegetables such as carrots or onions, a purée of vegetables, or stuffing into a turkey breast, turkey loaf, ham, or roast for flavoring and to create a colorful presentation when the meat is sliced.

lardons

Strips of fat used to **lard** meat or poultry, or to flavor certain dishes.

layer cake

A cake made up of several layers or tiers with a fruit preparation or sugar icing between the layers.

Tip: For a departure from the traditional cake that is completely covered with icing, put only a thin coating of icing between the layers, then just before serving, cover with fruit that has been lightly cooked in sugar syrup and perhaps flavored with liqueur. It's both elegant and a heck of a lot easier than icing a cake!

Another tip: To get an attractive, flat layer, trim off the top with a bread knife and arrange the layers upside down.

leaven, leavening

✺ An agent such as yeast or baking powder that causes dough to rise.

✺ To cause to rise by fermentation.

leek

An onion-like plant with a small bulb, white stem, and broad, flat leaves used mainly to flavor soups and sauces.

Be sure to trim off the fibrous green leaves and to wash leeks well to get rid of any residual grit.

legume See *beans*

lemon

A small, yellow citrus fruit with a sour pulp rich in ascorbic acid (vitamin C). Both the *zest* and juice are used extensively to enhance or add flavor to foods.

A lemon 'twist' is not just window dressing; twisting the zest or outer skin before adding it to a food or beverage releases the essential oils that contain the pleasant lemon flavoring and aroma. It's important when cutting the zest from a lemon for flavoring that all of the white pulp be removed so that its bitterness does not overpower the lemon oils.

lemonade

A beverage made from lemon juice, sugar, and water.

Tip: If it is too troublesome and expensive to make lemonade from scratch, try adding a bit of fresh lemon juice to the frozen concoction for better flavor and an extra shot of vitamin C.

126

Fresh lemon juice can add a spark of flavor to other juices and soda as well.

lemon butter

A combination of lemon juice and melted butter used as flavoring for seafood or vegetables.

lentil

The red or brown seeds of a member of the pea family shaped like flattened peas.

Rich in protein and virtually free of fat, lentils, like most beans, combine well with other foods. Flavored with onion, garlic, sweet peppers, etc. lentils make a hearty and healthy dish that goes well with meat or can substitute for it.

lettuce

Any of a number of leafy vegetables used mainly in salad.

The pale green leaves of iceberg tend to be our mainstay, but for a more distinctive flavor and improved nutrition, look to the darker green varieties.

Widely touted as a cancer preventive, lettuce does not have to be relegated to salad:

- Add chopped lettuce to soup.
- Mix chopped lettuce in other vegetable dishes.
- Lettuce should be chilled for storage, but it shouldn't be served directly from the refrigerator: leave it out for a few minutes to warm a bit so as to enhance the flavor and reduce the temptation to bathe it in calorific dressing; allow it to marinate in a light dressing for an hour or so to create a delicious wilted salad.

liaison

French—thickening. In English, a linking or connecting.

Think of the *liaison* as an ingredient or combination of ingredients that brings together and binds the elements of a sauce or dish.

lichee See *litchi*

Liebfraumilch

Originally, a monastic Rhine wine.

Commonly used to designate any Rhine-type wine, the name has become generic and is no guarantee of quality.

Liederkranz
Sounds very German, and it is... sort of. A strong, odoriferous and delicious version of **Limburger** created by a German-American around the turn of the century.

light cream
Cream that has risen to the top of whole milk after about twelve hours of standing; it is richer in butterfat than milk, but contains less than **whipping cream**.

light whipping cream
Cream from the top of whole milk that has been allowed to stand for over twelve hours. Light whipping cream has more butterfat than **light cream**, but less than **heavy cream**.

lima bean
As children, most of us are introduced to this flat green or white bean when forced to eat **succotash** or an insipid melange of mixed vegetables. Lima beans, however, can be a fine addition to a meal whether served solo with a bit of butter, or combined with sausage, onion, and cheddar cheese baked in white wine.

Limburger
This cheese is so closely associated with Germany that it is strange to learn that it originated in Belgium. Noted as well for its aroma, only a true believer even considers storing it in the refrigerator.
A more acceptable version of this cheese in most households is **Liederkranz**.

lime
A citrus fruit that looks like a small green **lemon**.
The lime has its own distinctive flavor, but everything we said about the lemon applies equally to the lime.

linguine
Pasta shaped like flattened spaghetti, supposedly to provide more surface for a sauce to cling to.
Linguine is usually served with a light preparation such as a thin clam or seafood sauce.

liquefy
To make into a liquid. Exactly how this is accomplished will depend on the recipe, your preference, and the tools you have at

hand. Simply straining and pressing out the juice usually won't do, as the term *liquefy* suggests that at least part of the solids will be incorporated into the liquid obtained.

A juicer, food processor, or blender will turn all but the most coarse foods into liquid or at least into a thin purée.

A food mill does not grind fine enough for most uses; however, we have on occasion used a food mill to grind such things as broccoli for cream of broccoli soup, then pressed the mixture through a fine sieve.

liqueur

A sweet alcoholic spirit flavored with fruit, nuts, spices, etc.

A few liqueurs are customarily served with coffee or in it after a meal, but most are used mainly as ingredients in mixed drinks or as flavoring for confections or fruit.

liquor

⚭ An alcoholic beverage made by the process of distillation.

⚭ Any liquid used in cooking or that results from cooking.

litchi, litchi nut

A fruit of Chinese origin, a bit larger than a cherry with a dark papery shell, a large pit, and sweet white meat.

liver

The largest of the glands in the digestive system of vertebrates comprising a delicate meat that requires little cooking.

Among those who dislike liver are the many victims of exposure to improper preparation of an overly strong-flavored liver, or to improper cooking that resulted in a tough, dry preparation that more nearly resembled the hide of the animal.

Other than *foie gras* which is most likely to be found in a *pâté*, the best liver is that of the chicken or calf. Baby beef is good, but the tough fibers should be removed before cooking. Liver from older beef as well as that from sheep or pork requires marinating to rid it of its strong flavor.

liverwurst

From the German *leberwurst;* literally, *liver sausage.* Liverwurst is made from liver finely ground to the consistency of a pâte.

loaf pan See *bread pan.*

lobster

The **American lobster** found along the east coast from Nova Scotia to North Carolina is a bottom-dwelling shellfish with ten legs, two of which have been modified to large claws. They survive well in salt water tanks and are often available fresh and live throughout the country.

The **spiny lobster** that lacks the large claws of the American lobster is fished from various locations around the globe and is usually served in the U.S. as *rock lobster* or *Florida lobster*. Spiny lobster deteriorate rapidly out of water and so must be frozen immediately after they are caught.

We've often speculated about who might have first discovered that the lobster is edible, for the creature certainly doesn't look appetizing. However, as any lover of fresh lobster will tell you, lobster is even more succulent than it is ugly.

loin

The front part of a hindquarter of beef, veal, lamb, or pork with the flank removed.

London broil

A broiled flank steak that is cut in thin slices diagonally across the grain and served with a rich gravy or sauce.

The flank is a flavorful cut, but not a tender one; the meat is sometimes marinated before cooking and should only be cooked rare for it toughens when cooked to medium or well-done.

lox

A type of smoked salmon; in fact, the premier smoked salmon. Lox are often served as an appetizer or garnish, but for some they only exist to accompany bagels and cream cheese at a breakfast or brunch.

Lyonnaise
Of a dish originated in, or prepared according to, the style of the Lyonnais district of France.

The region is noted for fine onions and so it is not surprising that most of the dishes we know as *Lyonnaise* are prepared with onions.

macaroni
A type of pasta, usually in the form of a short, curved tube about the circumference of a drinking straw.

Although lacking in hard data, we suspect that packaging which simplified preparation and advertising that targeted children have made macaroni and cheese one of the most popular made-at-home dishes in the U.S.

In addition, macaroni finds its way into summer salads, soups, and a variety of one-dish meals.

macaroon
A small cookie made of egg white and sugar, flavored with almonds or coconut.

mace
A spice ground from the dried shell of the **nutmeg**. This cinnamon-nutmeg flavoring is used mainly in marinades and sauces.

Madeira
Any of several types of premium **apéritif** wines made from grapes grown on the Portuguese island of Madeira.

maison
French—house; in a restaurant, often designating a specialty of the house or the chef. Such a designation should be limited to a dish made completely in house from a recipe created by the chef or restaurateur but, alas, such is not often the case.

malt
Grain such as barley that has been sprouted and dried for use in the brewing process.

mandarin, mandarin orange
A type of small, sweet Chinese orange.

mandolin

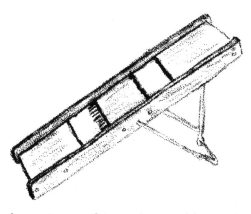

A device more commonly found in commercial kitchens than in the home, comprising a flat cutting surface that is four to five inches wide and twelve to fourteen inches long. One end of the mandolin has legs that prop the cutting surface up at about a 30° angle, leaving a space beneath for cut food to drop. A set of interchangeable cutting and grating blades provides the capability to cut food uniformly into slices, French fry strips, or into shreds.

A good mandolin can cost as much as a home food processor and we've noticed an interesting phenomenon in recent years—as professional chefs embrace the ease and convenience of the food processor, there seems to have come on the market for the home a number of inexpensive mandolin-type contraptions.

mango
A tropical fruit of the East Indies. Its orange flesh is eaten raw or used in the making of jams and Indian-style *chutney*.

manicotti
Italian—little muffs. A dish made by cooking thin sheets of pasta dough, placing any of a variety of preparations containing cheese, chopped meat, spinach, mushrooms, etc. in the center, then folding in the ends and rolling the dough to form those *little muffs* or pillows. The manicotti are then baked with sauce and grated cheese.

maple sugar
A sugar made by boiling down maple syrup.

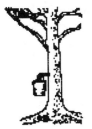

maple syrup
Syrup made by cooking sap drawn from the sugar maple.

Much syrup sold as *maple* contains little or no maple syrup, being comprised of sugar, water, and maple syrup flavoring, so check the label if you want real maple syrup.

maraschino
* A liqueur made from the black *marasca* cherry.
* Pitted cherries marinated in a syrup that is flavored with maraschino liqueur.

marble cake
A cake made from a combination of light and dark batters that are not thoroughly mixed together so as to create a marble-like appearance.

marbled
Descriptive of meat, usually beef, containing thin streaks of fat that have an appearance similar to the veins in marble; usually an indication of meat that will cook up moist and tender.

Marengo or Chicken Sauté à la Marengo
A dish of sautéed chicken, garnished with fried eggs and crayfish, and a sauce made from bread, oil, water, garlic, brandy, and tomatoes.

We have seen variations such as the *Chicken Marengo* described earlier in this book, but the ingredients listed here are purported to be those on hand and foraged from the countryside that were used in the preparation served to Napoleon after his victory at Marengo. According to legend, Napoleon was so delighted with the dish that he ordered it to be served after every battle. When the chef felt that the crayfish were out of place and substituted mushrooms, Napoleon was displeased, and so crayfish were reinstated as a part of the classic dish, although wine is generally substituted for the water.

margarine

A butter substitute made from refined vegetable oils.

Margarine has been touted as a healthy alternative to butter and it may be, but there are limitations: margarine does not taste the same as butter, nor does it flavor other foods or react to heat the same as butter, all elements that should be considered when making a substitution. That is not to suggest that margarine should not substitute for butter; only that allowances must be made.

On the lighter side, we saw a presentation purported to show the dangers of cooking with low-fat margarine that contains a high percentage of water. The margarine was placed in a very hot pan which immediately spit out steam and hot water. Frankly, we feel that anyone so foolish as to preheat a pan that much shouldn't be allowed near fire.

margarita

A cocktail of tequila, lime juice, sugar, and orange liqueur, served in a glass rimmed with salt.

marinade

A seasoned liquid that may be cooked or uncooked in which foods are steeped to preserve, flavor, or tenderize them.

Tip: A marinade doesn't have to be complicated: an inexpensive bottled French or Italian dressing is a great marinade for chicken that is to be baked or barbecued.

marinara

An Italian-style tomato sauce prepared without meat for serving over pasta or vegetables.

marinate

To steep in a *marinade*.

marjoram

Any of a group of plants of the mint family used to flavor soups, vegetables, or served fresh in salads.

marmalade

A preserve made by boiling down fresh fruit and often the rinds of orange, lemon, etc. with sugar.

marmite
- A large covered earthenware or metal cooking pot used mainly for cooking stock.
- A clear hearty broth, especially as developed in a marmite.

Marsala
An Italian fortified wine made from Sicilian grapes.

martini
A cocktail made from gin or vodka and dry vermouth, garnished with an olive or lemon twist.
See also, *gibson.*

marzipan
A confection of almond, sugar, and egg whites that is often colored and molded into various shapes.

masher
A simple device for crushing and blending vegetables. The task is now often carried out by the ubiquitous electric hand mixer that performs so well, especially for making a smooth purée, but for many the masher is still the dominant tool.

matzo
A crisp unleavened wafer made from water and flour.

mayonnaise
A cold sauce that is an *emulsion* of egg yolks and oil. Most have become so acclimated to the taste and tex-

ture of commercial mayonnaise that fresh-made seems like an entirely different condiment. Concern about the presence of harmful bacteria in raw eggs has further served to discourage the making of mayonnaise at home.

It is well to note that fresh mayonnaise does need to be handled carefully, for it can become deadly without any apparent sign of spoilage. Commercial mayonnaise is less a problem. We have often been critical of the tendency to make quality and flavor secondary to the interest of mass production; however, in this instance we must accede that the alteration of flavor by the addition of vinegar and other preservatives is preferential to playing a form of kitchen Russian roulette each time we eat. Nevertheless, the same care should be taken to refrigerate mayonnaise as with any fish, meat, or fowl that is to be served cold.

Tip: For a change of pace, serve mayonnaise that has been flavored with other ingredients:
- For a lighter flavor, mix with sour cream.
- To serve with cold fish or vegetables, add dill weed.
- Add minced tomato or some cold tomato sauce to serve with poultry or meat.
- Mix in a bit of ground or prepared mustard to serve with cold fish or sausage.

measuring

The measuring of ingredients can be something of an anomaly, from that of the free spirit who casually throws together ingredients to make exciting marinades but can't get a cake to rise properly, to the by-the-book cook who foregoes the preparation of a dish for want of a teaspoon of chives. The point is that to be creative and competent, one needs only to know what elements are critical. Making baked goods, emulsions, and gelatins often requires careful measurement of ingredients, time, and temperature, whereas many classic dishes have been created by the necessity of making do with the ingredients at hand.

measuring cup, measuring spoon

Anyone reading the previous entry will understand the importance of a good set of measuring tools. The world is full of cute stuff and gadgets, but for function be sure to have a set of that works for you. Anyone who hesitates to use those that are part of a wall decoration should buy a cheap, functional set as well.

Plastic utensils should be avoided, as they often retain oils. Metal is best if they are usually washed in a dishwasher.

meat

Once used to describe foodstuffs in general, meat now often denotes only red meat such as beef; or red meat and poultry; or red meat, poultry, and seafood.

In this day of creeping vegetarianism, it is prudent to be sure just what an invited guest means when he or she says, 'no meat'—some eschew products obtained from animals such as milk and eggs as well as the flesh of the animal.

meatball

A portion of ground meat shaped into a small ball.

We tend to associate meatballs with Italian cookery, but they are a popular foodstuff in a number of cuisines throughout Europe, especially in Austria and Germany.

Meatballs may be made from any meat or combination of meats and served separately, in a sauce, or in soup. If you are fortunate enough to have a *meat grinder*, leftovers can be ground to make small meatballs for a one-dish meal of noodles and vegetables—and who will ever suspect they are leftovers?

meat grinder

Another casualty of the modern market that often provides meat ground to the buyer's specification, today's kitchen is unlikely to sport a meat grinder unless it was acquired for a special purpose such as for making sausage.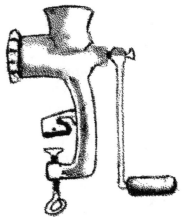

The meat grinder is a convenient tool, with interchangeable cutters that allow it to be used for a variety of tasks in much the same fashion as a *food mill*.

Tip: To get everything out of a meat grinder that was put into it, finish up with a slice of bread—as soon as the bread begins to show at the edge of the blades, you will know that all of the meat or other food has been pushed through.

meat loaf

Ground meat, often a combination of beef, pork, and veal, mixed with other ingredients, shaped into a loaf and baked.

Tip: For a fanciful touch, pack the bottom of a loaf pan with about one-third of the meat mixture, then spread strips of carrot, onion, pepper, other vegetables, or hard-boiled egg wedges over the mixture. Top with the rest of the meat mixture and bake. As well as adding flavor, when the loaf is cut, the flecks of color create an attractive presentation.

medallion

A small round of food, such as of beef (*tournedos*), veal, or pâté. Also called *collops* when applied to veal or pâté.

melon

Any of a variety of large fruit, such as the *cantaloupe*, *honeydew*, or *muskmelon*, with sweet flesh that mixes well with most other fruit.

melon baller

A kitchen tool designed to cut decorative balls from a melon.

Tip: Use the melon baller to cut rounds from apples, pears, or other fruit for appetizers or to embellish a salad plate, or from cooked potatoes, carrots, or other vegetables for garnish.

Another Tip: Use the melon baller to easily scoop the core from apple or pear halves.

meringue

A stiff mixture of egg white and sugar that is spread over the top of pastry and browned in the oven, or formed into various shapes and baked to used as decoration or as shells for filling. Meringue may be flavored and colored.

mesquite

A type of thorny shrub or tree common in the southwest and in Mexico, often used as a fuel for barbecuing food to which it imparts a distinctive flavor.

microwave, microwave oven

An appliance that cooks food quickly by piercing it with microwaves. Although the microwaves generate heat internally, they do not cook from the center without heating the outside as is popularly believed.

The oven is efficient for heating or cooking most food, but there are some **do's and don'ts**:

- Avoid using any container that absorbs microwaves; a good container allows most of the waves to pass through to heat the food. To test, fill the container with very cold water and cook for about one minute on high—if the container is warmer than the water it contains, don't use it.
- Avoid plastic containers as they tend to get hot from the food they contain and are likely to melt.
- Even a good microwave container may absorb heat from the food it contains—exercise care in removing hot food.
- The microwave tends to toughen baked goods such as bread or rolls—better to heat them in a conventional oven.
- And as you may have discovered, not all foods heat evenly or cook well in the microwave, so don't abandon the conventional oven.

Milanaise

Generally descriptive of a style of cooking that involves breading and sautéing in clarified butter.

milk

- A whitish fluid secreted by the mammary glands of a mammal; in American cookery, commonly the milk of the cow.
- Any similar fluid taken as food, such as coconut milk.
- To extract such a fluid from an animal or plant, as by *milking a coconut*.

See also *condensed milk, evaporated milk*.

millet
A cereal grain used for food throughout the world in somewhat the same manner as rice.
China is the world's leading producer of millet and though lacking statistics, we have it on good authority that as much millet is consumed in China as rice.

mimosa
* A traditional brunch cocktail comprised of chilled orange juice and champagne.
* Descriptive of a dish such as a salad or vegetable garnished with the chopped yolk of hard-boiled eggs.

mince
To chop in very small pieces.

mincemeat
A confection that is a combination of suet, fruit, sugar, spices, and meat that is marinated in brandy, rum, and Madeira; commonly used as filling for pie or tarts.

minestrone
An Italian soup of vegetables in a beef stock.
The ingredients of a minestrone vary according to the cook's preference, but the soup will invariably include tomatoes, and pasta, rice, or dried beans. Bits of beef or sausage may be added as well.

mint
Any of various aromatic leaves used for flavoring or garnish.

mirepoix
A mixture of lightly seasoned, diced carrots, onions, and celery, sometimes with ham, that is slowly cooked in butter and used to flavor other dishes or sauces.

miso
A fermented soybean paste used in Japanese cookery, especially in the making of soup.

mixer
Any device for combining and whipping foods.

Mixers range from the simple hand mixer that is also effective for chopping and blending soft foods such as cooked vegetables, to a heavy-duty machine mounted on a stand that may have attachments for performing additional tasks such as kneading dough, extracting juice or grinding meat.

See also **blender, egg beater, whisk.**

mocha

- ☀ A variety of fragrant coffee originally grown in Arabia.
- ☀ A flavoring mixture of coffee and chocolate.

molasses

A thick, dark liquid that remains after refining sugar, used in flavoring confections and in the distillation of rum.

mold

- ☀ A growth on the surface of food that indicates disintegration.
- ☀ To work into a particular shape or form.
- ☀ Hollow forms made from a variety of materials and in various configurations used to create decorative shapes or designs:
  - **Bread, cake, or pudding molds** of metal or earthenware are used to make decorative baked goods.
  - **Butter molds** are used to form blocks of butter into uniform bricks for storage or into a decorative shape for the table; smaller molds create pats of butter in a variety of patterns for individual service or for garnish.
  - **Candy molds** for bite-size or decorative pieces may be of metal or plastic, often in large sheets that contain a number of different forms. Two-piece molds are used to form larger shapes: the two halves are clamped together and filled through the base; when the candy has hardened, the halves are separated for easy removal.
  - **Cheese molds** are used both to shape cheeses when they are being made and to form cheese mixtures into a variety of shapes for the table.
  - **Gelatin or mousse molds** of copper are a traditional decoration in many kitchens, but not very practical for everyday

use: they must be lined so that the copper does not come in contact with food which may be adversely effected by it and the copper needs to be cleaned after each use if it is to be rehung as a decoration.

mollusk

In cookery, any of a group of edible, invertebrate, hard-shelled animals including escargot, clams, mussels, and oysters.

moonshine

Illegal whiskey, so-called because it is thought of as being distilled by the light of the moon.

morel

A flavorful mushroom that looks like a dark sponge. We are told that this is the only mushroom that does not have a poisonous counterpart; however, we are not inclined to test the hypothesis— as with all wild mushrooms we only eat those selected by an expert.

Mornay

- Mornay sauce; *béchamel* to which Gruyère and Parmesan cheeses have been added.
- Descriptive of a dish topped with Mornay sauce and usually browned under a broiler.

mortadella

An Italian sausage from Bologna, forerunner of the somewhat less elegant deli meat that came to this country named for that city where it also originated.

Mortadella is made from finely ground pork and beef pervaded with small cubes of pork fat and black peppercorns, flavored with spices, and smoked.

mortar

In cookery, a sturdy cup-like vessel in which ingredients such as herbs or spices are crushed with a *pestle*.

Moselle
A white wine made in the Moselle River valley of Germany or a wine claiming to be of that type.

mother
Mother of vinegar; a film that forms on the surface of vinegar, caused by bacterial action. The *mother* is used as a started in the making of vinegar.

moussaka
A Greek dish of layered pasta (macaroni or spaghetti), ground lamb in a thick, highly-seasoned tomato sauce, and a white sauce such as *Mornay*. Ingredients vary: eggplant is often mixed with the pasta or substituted for it, ground beef may replace the lamb, etc.
Regardless of the ingredients, the dish is baked in the oven, the white sauce on top is browned off, and the moussaka is cut into square or rectangular pieces for serving.

mousse
Any of a variety of preparations made light with beaten egg white or whipped cream and served cold.
A mousse may be an appetizer, a main dish or a side dish of seafood, meat, or vegetables; or it may be a pudding-like dessert containing fruit, chocolate, or other flavoring.

mousseline
A preparation such as a sauce that is lightened by the addition of whipped cream.

mozzarella
An Italian cheese with a smooth, firm texture and mild flavor.

muddle
To mix or blend. The term may also imply crushing, as when muddling fruit for a beverage or sauce.

muddler
The muddler can be a long rod for mixing beverages, or a short sturdy one shaped like a club used to crush ingredients.

Muenster
A mild American-style cheese with a smooth, firm texture that derives its name from a similar cheese that was first made in the area of Munster, France.

143

muffin

A light cake-like quick bread leavened with baking powder and baked in a small cup or mold.

Depending on its intended use, that is, for sweet or savory, the muffin may be sweetened or not and flavored with fruit or bits of meat such as bacon or ham.

muffin pan, muffin tin

A tray made up of six to twelve cup-like indentations about three inches in diameter, used to bake muffins, small dinner rolls, etc.

Tip: A muffin pan with a non-stick surface can be used to mold individual servings of gelatin or mousse. It can be handy for heating small quantities of vegetables or garnish in the oven as well.

mulligan stew

A *stew* made from a collection of meat and vegetables.

Characterized as a stew made up of bits and pieces of whatever food is available, mulligan stew is often prepared in a stock pot that is left simmering on the stove to collect food in season or leftovers.

mulligatawny

An East Indian soup of vegetables, lamb, and rice flavored with *curry*.

mushroom

Any of a large variety of fleshy fungi characterized by a stalk that is topped with an umbrella-like cap.

Only one who is knowledgeable about such matters should attempt to collect mushrooms in the wild, for it is generally agreed that there are no certain rules for distinguishing edible from inedible or even poisonous varieties. Similarly, none of the 'tests' such as the one claiming that poisonous varieties will blacken silver are effective either, except perhaps for one... A wag once suggested that a sampling of any dish containing mushrooms should first be fed to the cat; however, it seems foolish to pre-

144

pare a dish that may turn out to be inedible, and it could be hard on the cat. Not being experts, we generally confine ourselves to the cultivated varieties.

And a couple of other notes:

- Mushrooms keep best if they are not rinsed until just prior to cooking or serving.
- Mushrooms that have darkened may not appear appetizing, but their flavor has intensified and they are excellent when cooked, especially for soup.

muskmelon

- ✸ Any of a family of large fruit with rough skin and sweet meat such as the *cantaloupe*.
- ✸ Depending on the part of the country you hail from, *muskmelon* may be used to describe any melon.

mussel

An edible mollusk with an oblong, black shell. Mussels are almost always served cooked; their delicate flavor and texture can be best appreciated when they are lightly steamed and served in the shell, either as a separate dish or a garnish.

mustard

An herb of the same family as cabbage whose ground seeds are used as seasoning or mixed with liquid and other herbs or spices to make a condiment.

We haven't seen any claims that it is a cancer–preventive as are most other members of the cabbage family, but we love it anyhow.

Depending on how it is prepared, mustard may be relatively mild or extremely hot.

prepared mustard

Prepared mustard is simply dry mustard combined with a liquid to form a sort of paste; mixing with cold water, vinegar, wine or beer will produce a hot mustard, whereas heating the mixture will create a milder blend.

For an escape from ordinary commercial or 'ballpark' mustard, put together your own blend of mustard with garlic, onions or other flavoring.

Tip: Add a bit of prepared mustard to salad dressing, soup, or sauce to create a new flavor.

mutton

The strong-flavored meat from a grown sheep.

nacho
A crisp *tortilla* chip, often served with a sauce for dipping, or covered with a mixture of beans or ground meat and cheese.

napkin
A small square of cloth or paper used to protect clothing and to wipe the fingers and mouth when dining.

Before the *fork* became common at the dinner table, the napkin played a larger role and was correspondingly larger in size—used to wipe the knife after cutting meat as well as to cleanse the primary eating instrument, the fingers.

napoleon
A rich confection made up of layers of puff pastry and custard or other light filling.

navel orange
A hybrid seedless orange.

navy bean
A type of small white kidney bean that derives its appellation for almost two hundred years of honorable service as standard fare aboard naval vessels.

nectar
⁕ An elixir said to confer immortality, the name is commonly used to describe any beverage that is especially delicious.
⁕ The sweet fluid from flowers used by bees to make honey.

Neufchâtel
A soft white cheese similar in texture to cream cheese when unripened and that is yellowish and develops a skin when ripened.

Tip: Unripened Neufchâtel is similar in texture and color to cream cheese, but with thirty to forty percent less fat and a slight tang that is lacking in cream cheese—all in all, a healthy alternative that is gastronomically the better option as well.

neutral spirits

Ethyl alcohol that has been distilled to at least 190 proof. Neutral spirits are used to make vodka by the simple process of cutting with distilled water, and in the making of other alcoholic beverages by addition to adjust the alcohol content to the desired level.

newburg

* A rich cream and egg sauce flavored with shellfish and fortified wine.
* Descriptive of a dish prepared with a newburg-style sauce.

niçoise

* Descriptive of a number of dishes prepared with tomatoes and likely to be flavored with garlic. See *salade niçoise*.
* A cold sauce made by adding tomato purée, pimiento, and tarragon to mayonnaise.

noisette

* A small round of meat that is an individual portion.
* Potatoes cut into small spheres and lightly browned in butter.

Tip: Potatoes or carrots softened by boiling or steaming briefly are easily cut into *noisettes* with a *melon baller*.

noisette butter

Sweet butter that has been cooked to a light tan. The butter is always served while still hot and frothy.

nonpareil

* Multicolored granules of sugar used to decorate pastry.
* Small chocolate candies decorated with nonpareils.
* Small pickled capers.

noodle

A strip of broad, flat pasta dough that is added to soup, to baked casserole-type dishes, or served as a side dish.

nori

Thin sheets of dried seaweed that are used extensively in Japanese cookery to wrap preparations such as *sushi* or *sashimi*, or cut in thin strips for flavoring or garnish.

nosh
A snack, or to eat a snack.

nougat
A confection made from nuts and honey or thick sugar syrup, and sometimes containing candied fruit.

nouvelle cuisine
French—new kitchen or *new cooking*. A style of cooking popularized in the 1970's that emphasizes lighter food and sauces.
Nouvelle cuisine is something of a fusion between French and Oriental cooking that emphasizes fresh ingredients lightly cooked, sauces prepared by reduction rather than thickening, and artful presentation.

Nova
Short for Nova Scotia salmon, specifically **lox** made from that fish.

nut
The hard, edible seed and its woody outer covering that is characteristic of a variety of trees or shrubs such as the pecan or walnut.

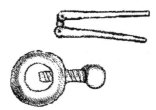

nutcracker
Commonly, a device consisting of two rods about six inches long joined at one end by a double hinge, designed to crack the hard shell of a nut. This type of nutcracker can also be used to crack the shells of lobster or king crab, but crackers designed specifically for that purpose are generally better suited to the task.
There are also a number of other creations used for this purpose such as a small wooden cup with a screw-like piece inserted through the side: the screw cracks the shell and the cup catches the pieces... or you may want to just settle for a hammer and a solid block of wood.

Tip: The hinged nutcracker is also a handy device for removing small stubborn screw-top lids.

nutmeg

Seed of the nutmeg tree that is ground and used as a spice. Fresh ground nutmeg is the best—whole nuts are readily available and keep indefinitely in the freezer. Anyone attached to gadgets will want a *nutmeg grater*, although most of us are content to use the finest blade of our all-purpose grater.

nutmeg grater

A small grater with fine cutting edges for reducing whole nutmeg to a fine powder.

Nutmeg graters range from simple flat or rounded panels designed only for shredding to more elaborate contraptions with a container for storing the whole nuts as well as a receptacle to catch the grated nutmeg.

nutritional yeast See *brewer's yeast*

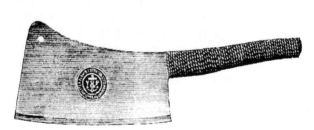

oatcake
A small, flat cake made from oatmeal.

oatmeal, rolled oats
Oats that have been ground or rolled for making breakfast cereal and other preparations.

It was easy to ignore oatmeal until we learned that it is an aid to lowering blood cholesterol. Now the only problem is finding time to prepare it and getting the family to eat it.

- *Quick-cooking oats,* (not *instant,* that may contain extra sodium) are the nutritional equal of their old-fashioned counterpart; the difference is in the way they are cut and of course the shorter cooking time. Cook oatmeal with a little butter, brown sugar, and cinnamon to make it more appetizing; vanilla, maple, or other flavoring can also help to turn the dish into a treat.
- Add quick-cooking oats to ground meat to extend it and make it a healthier food. The oats will soak up meat juices as well, so that extra flavor could be an additional reward.
- A small amount of oats added to soup will make it thicker and creamier.

offal
Pronounced *aw'ful* and it sounds like it is—the waste, mostly entrails, of a slaughtered animal.

Kudos to the public relations type who coined the phrase *variety meat* which sounds much more appetizing, for there are a host of delectable dishes made from the tongue, brains, tripe, liver and kidneys of an animal. It's just that we're not big fans.

oil
A fat, liquid at room temperature, obtainable from animal, vegetable, and mineral sources although for cooking most is obtained from vegetables.

Some information about oils:
- Cold-pressed oils retain the most nutrients and keep best.
- Olive oil is considered the 'healthiest', as it is reputedly not only low in cholesterol, but actually helps to lower LDL, the 'bad' cholesterol.
- Peanut oil is the best for deep-fat frying because it withstands high heat for long periods better than most oils.
- Nut oils (other than peanut oil) can add flavor to salads but they are generally unsuitable for cooking because they have a low smoking temperature.

oilstone

A type of sharpening stone.

okra

The pods of a tall plant grown in the south that are boiled or fried and eaten as a vegetable; one of the main ingredients in *gumbo*.

oleo

Short for *oleomargarine*. See *margarine*.

olive

The small oval fruit of a tree native to the eastern Mediterranean, picked when it is green (unripe) or black (ripe).

Most olives harvested go into the making of oil, but they are nonetheless available in abundance for condiment or garnish. Green olives are normally pitted and pickled, sometimes stuffed with a filling such as pimiento, almond, onion, or anchovy. Ripe olives may be pitted or not and processed in a number of ways, such as by drying or preserving in oil.

olive oil

The oil extracted from olives, long considered by chefs of the western world as the finest of all vegetable oils—in fact, the Latin word for *oil* applies only to olive oil.

The best olive oil is *cold pressed*, that is, extracted by pressure without the aid of heat. Cold-pressed olive oil has a more distinctive color and flavor than any other.

The second pressing is accomplished with the aid of heat that diminishes somewhat the quality of the oil. *Light* olive oil is the result of passing the oil through a fine filtration system that removes most of the characteristic color and flavor.

The particular qualities of an oil will vary depending on such things as where the olives are grown, when they are harvested, and the way in which they are processed, so it behooves the cook to seek out a brand or brands that best suit his or her particular taste. Most will want to keep on hand both cold pressed for dishes that benefit from the flavor of the oil, and light that is better for frying. All contain the same amount of monounsaturated fat that is said to be beneficial.

See also, *oil*.

omelet, omelette

Beaten eggs that are quickly fried and served folded over, often with a filling; a French omelet.

There seems to be a great mystique surrounding the making of a French omelet that involves using a pan reserved for that one purpose alone, lightly beating the eggs so as not to incorporate air into the mixture, then cooking briefly in a hot pan and turning out onto a plate while still runny. Purists may further insist that an omelet can only be made with three eggs, and that the 'filling' should not go into the egg in the pan, but only be placed over the omelet after it is finished cooking. To further confuse the cook in America, our idea of the perfect French omelet tends to a well-beaten concoction that arrives at the table browned and fluffy, somewhat like a soufflé.

Whatever your preference, here are some cooking tips:

- The pan must have angled sides and a smooth surface so that the omelet will slide out easily. Melt a bit of **clarified butter** or oil in the pan and swirl it around to completely coat the bottom and sides.
- The pan should be hot enough to bind the eggs as soon as they hit the surface, but not so hot as to scorch them. As soon as the eggs hit the pan, shake it briskly and stir the top of the eggs to spread them, taking care not to scrape the bottom of the pan. Those who want eggs cooked through may have to settle for lower heat or for browning off the mixture under the broiler.
- A fluffier omelet will result if a small amount of water is beaten with the eggs; for the ultimate high-riser, separate the eggs and gently fold together beaten yolks with slightly stiff whites.

- The portion of filling added to the eggs should be light so that it will be covered when the omelet is folded and to allow removal without breaking up. Saving a bit of the filling to top the omelet before serving is a nice touch.

Omelets can be filled or complemented with almost anything edible:

- Stuff with bits of cheese, chicken, chicken livers, ham, sausage, bacon, shellfish, anchovies, onion, peppers, asparagus, mushrooms, tomatoes, peas, carrots, spinach, or potatoes. Combine ingredients for variety. Omelet additions should be cut into fine dice or *julienne* and are usually cooked, although raw tomatoes are an interesting complement.
- Serve with a flavorful white, brown, or tomato sauce that has been spread on the plate with the omelet on top.
- For a heartier meal, cover a plate with sauce, then top it with an omelet and a chicken breast, sausage or full portion of the ingredients used in the filling.

Just for the record, we often apply the term *omelet* to other similar egg dishes such as the **frittata** from Italy, Chinese **egg foo yung** or the American **western omelet**, all of which combine filling and eggs before cooking.

onion

The edible bulb or leaves of a member of the lily family, having a sharp taste and aroma.

Onion generally refers to the large bulb sold without leaves, whereas the small bulb with long green leaves is called a *scallion* or *green onion*. Certain varieties, such as the *Vidalia onion* are prized for their mild, sweet flavor. These are especially good raw, but may be lacking that distinctive onion bite and taste a bit too sweet for many dishes when cooked.

Onions can be prepared in a variety of ways, but are mostly used to augment the flavor of other dishes. Whether served alone or added to other preparations, for a mild flavor, sauté lightly until just translucent; for a stronger flavor, continue until golden brown; and for full flavor, as for onion soup, brown them, but do it slowly taking care not to scorch and make them bitter.

Tip: Add a bit of onion, fried or boiled according to your preference, to add flavor to vegetable dishes.

Peeling and cutting onions without discomfort seems to be a never-ending problem for which there seems to be a never-ending list of solutions. Some suggestions call for dipping onions briefly into boiling water, placing them in the freezer for a few minutes before cutting, affixing a chunk of fresh bread to the end of the knife, slicing from the stalk end back to the root, and cutting under running water. As the problem is one of an irritating substance that is released into the air and finds its way to the eyes, we're just silly enough to offer our own suggestions:
- Begin with a sharp knife—a dull one tears at the flesh of the onion and promotes the release of irritants.
- Rinse and leave the onion, knife and cutting board wet—water seems to absorb the irritant.
- Rinse the knife and uncut portion of onion again at the first hint of discomfort and as often as necessary during the process—once the eyes start to burn there is no alternative but to walk away and find fresh air. (And heed your mother's advice not to rub your eyes!)

Tip: Onions that are overly strong but not spoiled may be especially good in soup, but too hard to handle to get them there. Tone them down by steaming or boiling a bit and allowing them to cool before slicing and browning. Save the water to add to the soup after the onions are browned.

Stuffed onions
Try this to dress up a plate: Cut the top and bottom from medium-sized onions. Blanch or steam them just until soft enough to push out the center leaving two or three solid outer layers. Combine the onion centers, finely chopped with ground meat, sausage, or your favorite dressing and stuff the onion shells with the mixture. Place them in a buttered oven pan and bake (time will vary according to the stuffing), basting often with thin brown gravy.

orange

A citrus fruit with a reddish-yellow outer skin, a bitter white inner skin, and usually sweet, reddish-yellow pulp.

The skin is used as a garnish and to flavor certain dishes, confections, and liqueurs. The pulp is similarly used as garnish or flavoring, or consumed as a fruit or the juice extracted from it.

oregano

A plant of the mint family similar to marjoram used to flavor soups, meat, and vegetables.

orgeat

A flavoring syrup made from almonds.

osso buco

A knuckle of veal baked with white wine and tomato. Unfortunately, that simple description does not do justice to this wonderful delicacy of meat and marrow.

ouzo

A Greek liqueur flavored with anise. The clear liquid turns a milky color when mixed with water, its usual accompaniment.

oven

An enclosed area capable of sustaining high heat for cooking.

It is only when we reflect on ovens used in the past that we recognize what a marvelous device we have to work with today. Consider the difficulty of sustaining a constant temperature when cooking in a fireplace niche that was first heated with coals and then used for baking after the coals were removed, or of firing an oven with wood that gave off uneven heat.

It is important to know that even a modern oven is performing properly. Use an oven thermometer to make certain that the thermostat shuts down the heat source at the proper temperature; if it doesn't, it may be replaced or, if the temperature is consistently high or low, you may be able to compensate by setting the temperature dial accordingly. To check for hot spots, place a small oven-proof dish such as a custard cup filled with water near each corner and heat without bringing the water to a boil. Check each with a food thermometer; a significant difference in temperature is a good indicator that no award-winning cakes will be baked in that oven.

oven-proof

An imprecise classification of cookware indicating that it is satisfactory for use in the oven. Such a designation is often a clear warning not to subject the utensil to direct heat, although in some cases it may indicate that a pan normally used on the stovetop is adequate for limited use in the oven, such as for browning.

It is always safest to read the manufacturer's instructions that may set a limit to the amount of heat that the material can withstand without damage.

ovenware

Cookware designed for use in the oven. For glass and earthenware, observe the same precautions as for *oven-proof*.

oyster

* The oval portion of tender meat contained in a bone depression near the back of a fowl.
* A tender, succulent bivalve mollusk that may be eaten raw or in various preparations.

  Although frowned on by those concerned about pollutants in the water; die-hards seem generally unwilling to give up the pleasure of eating fresh-shucked oysters raw. Fortunately or unfortunately, most of us are not faced with that dilemma, for packaged oysters lack the special quality of freshly-shucked and are just as well steamed.

  Preparations range from simple steamed, poached, or grilled oysters served with a topping of Parmesan cheese or sauce, to complex dishes that include a variety of ingredients.

Oysters Rockefeller

Baked oysters served on the half shell covered with a purée of spinach, onion, bacon, and seasonings flavored with anisette.

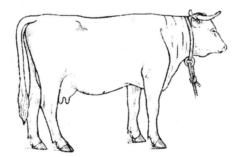

paella

A rice-based one-dish meal of Spanish origin that takes its name from the iron pan in which it is cooked and served. The paella pan is like a large frying pan that has two handles in order to heft the heavy contents.

Ingredients vary according to availability and the customs of the region in which it is made, but a paella will usually contain in addition to rice, small pieces of beef, ham, or sausage, a cut-up chicken, tomatoes, onions, peppers, kidney beans, peas, and fish, flavored with saffron. In areas where they are available, the dish will often be topped with fresh mussels, shrimp, or lobster, all steamed and served in their shells.

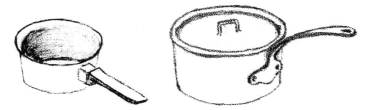

pan

Any of a variety of vessels used for cooking and often described in more specific terms such as *frying pan*, *saucepan*, etc.

pancake

A thin cake made from batter fried in a pan or on a griddle; a flapjack or griddlecake.

The French would call it a *crêpe*, but Americans differentiate between the thin French version that often holds a filling and these thick cakes that may constitute the main part of a meal.

pan fry

Generally, a less pretentious term for sauté, although often referring to a preparation that requires longer and slower cooking in a frying pan.

pan gravy

* The liquids left in a pan after cooking.
* A thick sauce made from the fat and juices extracting during cooking.

papaya

An oblong topical fruit with meat much like a melon.

paprika

'Hungarian sweet pepper' says one of our references; 'frequently hot' says our experience with the cooking of a Hungarian friend. A red pepper used extensively in Hungarian cooking that may be either sweet or hot, but never so hot as the chili or cayenne. Paprika does not take kindly to heat, so it should only be added to a dish that is finished or nearly finished cooking if it is to remain bright red and flavorful.

parbake, parboil

To partially cook food; usually one stage of a complex recipe that requires addition preparation before cooking is completed.

pare

To trim or cut away the peel or outer layer.

parfait

Originally, a frozen mixture of eggs, sugar, whipped cream, and flavoring usually served with syrup. Now often used to describe a dessert of layered ice cream, fruit, syrup, liqueur, etc. served in a tall stemmed glass.

paring knife
A small knife used for peeling or trimming.

Parmentier
For Antoine-Auguste Parmentier who popularized potatoes as food in France near the end of the eighteenth century; descriptive of a preparation that includes potatoes.

Parmesan, Parmigiano
A hard Italian cheese used extensively in the flavoring of sauces and other preparations. The dry grated stuff in a box is in no way comparable to freshly grated that is equally at home flavoring and thickening a white or red sauce, as a flavoring for vegetable dishes, or a seasoning for bread crumbs in a gratin.

parmigiana, parmigiano
Descriptive of a dish prepared with Parmesan cheese.

parsley

An aromatic herb with curled leaves used to season preparations or garnish dishes. Parsley is noted for its ability to freshen the breath, especially after eating garlic or onions.

parsnip
A root vegetable similar to the carrot, although white in color, served as a vegetable or used to flavor soup stock.

passion fruit
The egg-like fruit of a tropical American tree used mainly for its sweet juice.

pasta

A dough or paste made from flour, water, and eggs that is formed and prepared in a variety of ways.

Most pasta is made from *semolina*, a coarse durum wheat flour that is more glutinous than all–purpose flour which helps the pasta to retain its shape. Pasta shapes may be:

- small pieces such as **orzo** and **pastina**.
- long round strands such as **angel hair**, **spaghetti**, **spaghettini**, and **vermicelli**.
- flat strands such as **fettuccine** or **linguine**.
- tubes such as **macaroni**, **mostaccioli**, **penne**, and **ziti**.

Often pasta is stuffed such as for **cannelloni**, **manicotti**, **ravioli**, and **tortellini**. Some pasta such as **cavatelli** or **shell** may be stuffed or not. Other pasta seems designed for a single purpose such as **lasagna** noodles that are broad and flat so as to easily form a layer in a baking dish.

For the uninitiated and adventurous: be aware that this is only a sampling of pasta types, for every region of Italy has its collection of unique plain and stuffed pasta shapes and sizes; look for varieties newly available in the market and try them for a change. You may also want to get out of the tomato sauce rut, as delicious as it is, and try dressing pasta with white or brown sauce or gravy, or something simpler, such as butter, garlic, fresh herbs, or cheese.

Tip: Cooking time for pasta varies according to type, whether it is fresh or dried, and to some extent, its age. Package directions are a helpful guide, but the only way to tell if pasta is truly done to individual taste is by testing.

pasta primavera

A dish of spaghetti or linguine mixed with a colorful array of vegetables in a light sauce.

pasteurization

A process whereby harmful bacteria is arrested or destroyed by heating a liquid and holding it at a designated temperature for a specified amount of time.

pastrami

Highly seasoned corned beef that is smoked; a deli meat traditionally made into a sandwich with rye bread and mustard.

Tip: One more turkey substitute that found its way to market is turkey pastrami: it won't ever dupe anyone into thinking that it's beef, but with the spicy flavoring of pastrami intact, it is a pleasant alternative for those who want to cut down on their consumption of red meat.

pastry

* A dough or paste of flour, water, eggs, and shortening often used to make the crust for a pie or pâté.
* Baked confections made from pastry dough.

pastry bag

A cone-shaped cloth bag with an opening at the small end to accommodate a *pastry nozzle*.

The pastry bag and nozzle are used to *pipe* ingredients decoratively over a preparation.

pastry blender

A hand-held device with several projecting loops of wire used to blend dry and liquid ingredients for pastry dough. The pastry blender is also useful for combining other foods such as butter and sugar for cookie dough.

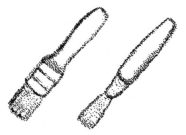

pastry brush

A brush not unlike a small paint brush used to coat pastry with beaten egg, milk, melted butter, syrup, etc. The brushes have many other uses around the kitchen as well such as for oiling baking pans or coating meat with a marinade before cooking.

Tip: The brushes wash easily in warm soapy water and should be hung to dry in the air. When used for eggs, however, be sure to rinse first in cold water or the result may be a brush that is permanently egg battered.

pastry nozzle

A cone-shaped metal fitting that is inserted into the end of a **pastry bag** or affixed to a syringe for piping decorative strips of icing or other food.
See also, *pipe*.

pâte

Pronounced *pat*, the French word for all manner of dough, batters, or pastes.

pâté

Pronounced *pa-te´*, a meat or fish dish encased in pastry and that is served hot or cold.
Pâté is traditionally made in a long pan about half the height and width of our traditional bread loaf pan. The smaller size facilitates slicing and serving as well as making a fine presentation.
The pâté and its sister the *terrine* which is baked in a casing of bacon instead of pastry are not common on the American table, perhaps because of the seeming difficulty of preparation. It is certain, however, that a creative cook armed only with a small loaf pan and some deli ham slices to line it could create a blend of meat and potatoes for filling and thus furnish a glorious end to otherwise nondescript leftovers.

pâté de foie gras

Probably the most famous of pâtés, a preparation of goose liver baked in a light pastry crust.

164

patty
- A small, flat, round of food; often ground food such as the ubiquitous *hamburger patty*.
- A small pie, especially one filled with meat or vegetables.

pea
A small, round, usually green, seed or bean that is eaten as a vegetable.

Peas are considered very nutritious because of their low fat and sodium content coupled with a good helping of soluble fiber that aids in lowering blood cholesterol and preventing cancer.

Tip: Tired of plain old peas on the plate? Dress them up and flavor them with some sautéed mushrooms or onion. Or add some color with bits of pimiento or pine nuts.

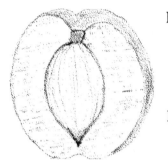

peach
A fruit of Chinese origin with yellow to red skin and sweet, reddish-yellow flesh that is eaten raw or used in the making of syrups, beverages, and numerous desserts.

peanut
A nut indigenous to America that is generally eaten boiled or roasted, or made into peanut butter or peanut oil.

peanut butter
A thick spread made from pulverized peanuts.

Although commercial brands may contain as much as 10% added sugar, oil, and salt, 'natural' styles with no additives are becoming more readily available. These too may be somewhat lacking in nutritional value if the germ has been removed to prolong shelf life.

For the absolutely best peanut butter, although perhaps not as smooth as the store brand, try making it from fresh roasted nuts in a food processor—you may have to add a little oil to get the mixture started.

peanut oil
Oil pressed from peanuts; the preferred oil for most cooking and deep frying as it has a high smoking point and is odorless and tasteless.

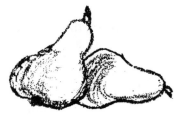

pear
Any of a variety of a fruit with a bulbous base that tapers to a top portion about the size of an egg with skin color ranging from pale yellow to red, and white or yellowish-white flesh.
Pears are eaten raw or cooked (see following), used in the making of a variety of pastries and in flavoring liqueur.

poached pears
For those who love pears, but tire of the hard fruit served up in most markets, or just for an elegant touch to end a meal. Halve pears, peeled or not, according to preference and remove the core (a melon baller does this job well); place in a buttered baking dish and sprinkle with syrup, cinnamon, jelly, etc.; allow to bake in a moderate (350°) oven until tender. Serve garnished with a sprig of mint or edible flowers.

pearl onion
A small, mild onion about the size of a cherry used mainly as a garnish or in making creamed onions.

pecan
A smooth-shelled nut shaped like a large olive. It's flesh looks like that of the English walnut to which it is related. The pecan is used extensively to flavor confections.

peel
- The outer covering of a fruit or vegetable.
- To remove the skin or rind from a fruit or vegetable.

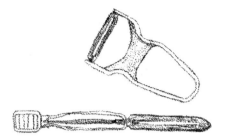

peeler

A cutting tool designed to slice in thin layers or to remove the peel from vegetables.

Tip: The peeler is also a handy device for making carrot curls, or for making thin slices as a first step to cutting *julienne* strips.

pekoe

A type of black tea from Sri Lanka and India.

pepper

⊛   Any of a group of pod-like fruits used mostly to flavor other dishes, such as the bell or green pepper, pimiento, chili pepper, or jalapeño.

⊛   Any of a variety of spices used in cooking such as paprika, cayenne, or chili.

⊛   Black pepper, a condiment.

peppercorn

The dried berry of a pepper plant, especially black pepper.

pepper mill

A device for grinding peppercorns such as those of black pepper; commonly used in the kitchen or at the table.

Owning a pepper mill won't change your life, but it will change your concept of what ground pepper tastes like.

peppermint

An aromatic plant of the mint family from which oil is extracted for flavoring confections, liqueurs, etc.

pepperoni

A spicy *summer sausage*.

pepper pot

Any of several types of spicy *stew* that may contain meat, seafood, or tripe, and vegetables.

pepper steak

* See *steak au poivre*
* A Chinese preparation of beef and green pepper strips that are stir fried and served with a sauce.

pestle

A sturdy rod that is shaped like a club for crushing ingredients, as in a *mortar*, or tapered for forcing food through a *sieve* or *chinois*.

pesto
A purée of fresh basil, garlic, pine nuts, and Parmesan cheese mixed with olive oil and commonly served over pasta.

petite marmite

- A small covered earthenware container for serving consommé; it is a replica of the larger vessel in which the broth is prepared.
- An individual serving of consommé that traditionally includes the ingredients that make up the dish such as bits of meat, poultry, marrow bones, stock pot vegetables, etc.

petit four
A small ornate cookie or iced cake.

pewter
Any of various tin alloys used in the making of tableware and decorative pieces.

phosphate
A soda fountain drink of syrup, charged water, and sometimes milk. So-named because the drink originally contained a few drops of phosphoric acid.

phyllo
Rich pastry dough in very thin sheets that are combined to make layers of light, flaky crust for a variety of preparations.

picante
Descriptive of a cold sauce that is spicy, typically one whose main ingredients are tomato, pepper, and onion.

piccalilli
A mustard pickle relish that is made up from a variety of chopped vegetables.

pickle
Any food that is preserved in a solution of brine or vinegar.

pie

☀ A preparation that is baked with a pastry crust.
In the U.S., the word *pie* almost always conjures up a vision of sweets; throughout Europe it is just as likely to evoke memories of a hearty dish of beef, pork, or fowl. And for real men secure enough to eat *quiche*, it too is a type of pie.

☀ Any dish similar to pie such as one of pudding with a shell of crumbs that is not baked, or of meat with a top crust of mashed potato that may be baked or top browned such as *shepherd's pie.*.

pie crust

A light, flaky crust used in the making of pies, tarts, and other pastries.

pie pan, pie dish

A round, square, or oblong pan or dish in which a pie is contained.

The pan or dish may be of glass, metal or earthenware. A dessert pie is likely to be prepared in a relatively shallow pan whereas a more robust pie of savory is usually made in a deep dish that is also the container used in the making of traditional English puddings.

pilaf, pilau

Rice cooked in a seasoned broth, often with other ingredients such as finely-cut vegetables, meat, or shellfish.

pilsener, pilsner

A light, dry *lager* that is typically bland unlike the Czech Pilsner Urquell that is the original pilsner.

pimiento

A mild red pepper used primarily for garnish and as flavoring in certain dishes.

Tip: For a colorful appetizer or side dish, stuff whole pimientos with creamed peas or with julienne strips of vegetables garnished with mayonnaise to which a bit of sour cream, dill weed, or mustard has been added.

pineapple
A native American plant with a rough yellow-brown exterior that masks the sweet, tasty, yellow fruit of its interior. Few who have fallen victim to the convenience of opening cans miss as much as those who have never taken the trouble to peel a fresh ripe pineapple to savor the succulent meat within.

Tip: Use a whole, fresh pineapple as the centerpiece for a buffet studded with toothpicks containing bite-size pieces of fruit or cheese. Cover the plate on which it sits with more food or with small blossoms.

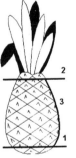

peeling a pineapple
Method 1, for a whole pineapple: Trim off the bottom (1) and top (2), taking care when handling the prickly leaves. Use a coring tool or a sharp knife with a long, thin blade to remove the core. With the fruit still in an upright position remove the rind by slicing from top to bottom (3) following the contours of the fruit. Use the tip of a knife or corer to remove any of the 'eyes' that remain in the fruit.

Tip: A whole pineapple, trimmed and cored makes an attractive and flavorful addition to a punch bowl. The marinated fruit can be served later as part of a fruit cocktail.

Method 2, for slices or pieces: Trim off the top and bottom, then remove the rind as above. For chunks, cut away large pieces avoiding the core; for slices, cut into slices first, then remove the core with a round biscuit or cookie cutter.

pine nut

The soft, edible seed of certain pine trees used as an ingredient in salad and other dishes. Also listed variously as *pignoli, pignon, piñon,* or *pinyon.*

pinto bean

A hearty bean shaped like a kidney bean with a mottled black and yellow-white coloring, used especially in Mexican-style dishes such as chili.

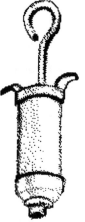

pip, pippin

The small seed of a fleshy fruit such as of the orange or apple.

pipe

To decorate or garnish by forcing a stiff mixture such as icing, meringue, mashed potatoes, etc. through a pastry nozzle with the use of a *pastry bag,* syringe (shown on the left), or similar device.

pirogi, peroghi, piroshki, pirozhki

We're offering all the spellings we could find so as not to enter into debate about which is correct, or for that matter, which are made in individual serving size and which are large enough to be cut into portions. Our experience is limited to the hospitality of a friend who introduced us to the small pastries that are filled with cheese, meat, or mashed potatoes and eaten out of hand.

pistachio

A small nut having a very hard, smooth, light brown shell that splits open when roasted to reveal an oily, greenish-yellow kernel of exquisite flavor. Pistachios are used to flavor both sweet and savory dishes.

pita

A flat bread of the Middle East that has gained great popularity in this country as pocket bread that can hold a variety of foods.

pitter See *cherry pitter*

pizza
A round or square of dough that is traditionally topped with tomato sauce, cheese, and other ingredients.

Surprise—here's another plea to get out of a rut—try brushing a round of pizza dough with a little oil, then topping it with seasoned vegetables or meat and cheese, with fruit, or with honey and nuts. Works pretty well on pita bread too!

plank
To broil or bake and serve meat or fish on a wooden board.

The plank should be of a type intended for this purpose, marked with grooves to capture the juices from cooking. Food prepared in this manner takes on a bit of flavor from the wood.

plantain
A tropical fruit similar to the banana, but somewhat larger. Plantains are only eaten cooked, as a vegetable.

planter's punch
A tall rum drink, the recipe for which varies according to the whim of the mixologist or the drinker. Basically it is comprised of rum, lime juice, sugar, and carbonated water to which lemon, orange, or pineapple juice and Triple Sec may be added according to taste.

plat du jour
French—specialty of the day; often a pretentious means for an otherwise nondescript eating establishment to describe the blue plate special.

plate
A shallow dish that may be used for an individual serving, to hold food to be served, or simply for decoration.

The plate in one form or another has been around for some time; examples date from ancient Greece and Rome although it is likely that the common people had to settle for wooden bowls. The individual plate fell into disuse in the early Middle Ages, and was replaced by a thick round of bread called a *trencher*.

By the eleventh century it became customary to seat a nobleman and lady together at a banquet so as to share a common plate and goblet, but it is unlikely that the general populace found it convenient to give up the practice of eating directly from a serving dish or platter.

Even among the gentry plates were not plentiful as they had to be individually made and so visitors often carried their own service. It was not until the eighteenth century that mass-produced plates and other tableware were introduced and it became somewhat more common for a host of means to own a complete table setting.

In time all of this grandeur sifted down to the commoners so that today we find it surprising if a household does not have at the very least place settings for four.

plum

Any of a large variety of fruit about the size of a lemon with a smooth skin, edible pulp, and a single large stone. Most are edible as fresh fruit and are widely used in the making of desserts, preserves, and sauces.

plum pudding

There is no fruit of the plum tree in plum pudding; however, raisins, when baked into such a pudding or cake are called *plums*. Some plum puddings may be baked, but the traditional English Christmas pudding made up of raisins, currants, spices, and stout, brandy or sherry, and that may contain other fruit or their juices, bound together with flour, eggs, and suet is steamed for several hours. Once cooked, the pudding is stored in a cool place for at least three months before it is considered ready to eat, so plan ahead!

poach

To cook in a simmering liquid.

poached egg

No big trick here, as long as the water is just at the boiling point and the egg is cracked into a cup or shallow bowl so that it can be slid gently into the water.

Baste the top of the egg with the water to cook evenly, or for well-cooked, put a lid on the pan for a couple of minutes.

We have seen suggestions for pouring a little vinegar into the water—sounds nasty and is nasty unless one likes the aroma of vinegar with eggs.

For a change, poach the eggs in broth or a thin soup; serve in a small bowl on toast rounds and pour the broth over.

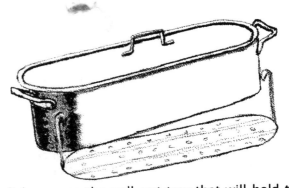

poached fish
When poaching fish, grease the pull-out tray that will hold the fish; if the pan does not have such a tray, grease the pan and lay the fish on a layer of cheesecloth long enough to hand over the ends of the pan for easy removal. Place the fish in the pan and barely cover with water, broth, wine, or flat beer. A whole fish should be started in cold liquid; for fillets or steaks, the liquid may be boiling. If the pan is to be covered, leave an opening to prevent steam from building up and overcooking the fish; by far the best method is a lid of parchment paper cut to the size of the pan and vented in the center to allow the release of steam.

pole bean
A type of large green bean grown on vines supported by poles.

polenta
A cornmeal porridge similar to grits with Parmesan cheese added that is chilled in a loaf pan after cooking, then sliced and fried. Polenta may be an accompaniment to a meat dish or served with a tomato or meat sauce

pollack
A north Atlantic fish; a species of *whiting* with sturdy flesh similar to the cod. Pollack is used extensively in the commercial preparation of fish and chips, and in *faux* preparations, such as fake crabmeat or lobster.

polonaise
A style of preparation that calls for garnishing with crumbled hard-cooked egg yolk and *noisette butter*.

popover
A type of unleavened muffin with a medium-brown outer shell and a hollow core that is made with flour, eggs, milk, and butter.

poppy seed
The tiny dark seed of the poppy, used mainly in baked goods as a flavoring or sprinkled over bread loaves.

pork
The meat from a pig or hog. Pork is a fine example of the power of good press. Formerly best known and often shunned for its reputedly high fat content—spareribs, bacon, sausage, etc.— pork is now touted as a healthy meat by the industry which cites Department of Agriculture figures that claim lean cuts contain little more fat than chicken.

port
A robust, sweet, fortified wine. Brandy is added to the wine to halt fermentation after which it is aged and blended. Younger wines are sold as *ruby port*; those aged further are classified as *tawny port.*

potato
A brown- or red-skinned tuber of South American origin.
Introduced into various parts of Europe during the middle of the sixteenth century, potatoes did not become a significant food there until a hundred years later. In the U.S. the potato has become as important to the table as pasta is to the Italian.
For those concerned about health, potatoes are low in fat and sodium, a significant source of fiber credited with lowering blood

cholesterol, and of potassium reputed to reduce the chance of stroke.

Unfortunately, the way in which we prepare and serve potatoes negates much of the good: we tend to destroy up to 50% of the potassium content by boiling them, then add sodium and fat in the form of salt and butter when we serve them.

To right these wrongs if they are of concern, steam or bake the potato, then serve with sour cream which has 25% of the fat contained in butter or margarine, and season with lemon pepper or some other salt substitute.

potato masher

A kitchen utensil for mashing potatoes and other vegetables. Depending on design, the masher may also double as a pastry blender.

pot-au-feu

A method of preparation in which meat and vegetables are boiled, then the broth strained and served separately.

pot cheese

A type of cottage cheese with a large, dry curd.

potholder

❋ A heavy fabric pad or glove used to handle hot utensils.
❋ A hanger for a pot or group of pots.

pot liquor

The liquid left in the pot after meat or vegetables are cooked, often used to make gravy.

potpie

❋ A deep-dish meat or poultry pie baked with a top crust.
❋ A kind of meat or poultry stew topped with dumplings.

pot roast

❋ A method of cooking meat slowly in a covered pan to which minced vegetables have been added for flavoring.
❋ Meat that has been cooked in this fashion.

pot stickers
Small dumplings filled with seafood, meat, or vegetables that are simmered in broth and served as appetizers in Chinese cuisine.

pottage
Once a kind of porridge; now used to describe a thick soup or stew of vegetable and meat.

potted
- Description of food preserved in a pot or similar container.
- Often used to describe food marinated in vinegar or some other liquor.

poulard, poularde
A young hen fattened for the table.

poultry
Any domesticated fowl such as chicken or ducks raised for meat or eggs.

poulty shears See *kitchen shears*

pound cake
- Originally a rich cake made from a pound each of flour, sugar, and butter.
- Any similar cake that is rich in flavor and texture.

pousse–café
A drink made from several liqueurs that are carefully layered in a glass.
The trick to making a pousse-café is in knowing the relative density of all the ingredients so that they can be layered one atop the other without blending.

powdered sugar
Sugar that has been pulverized into fine particles, used mainly in the making of confections.

praline
- A patty of candy made from chopped almonds or pecans and brown sugar or maple syrup.
- An almond coated with sugar that may be variously colored and flavored.

Can't resist the opportunity to avoid confusion (or add to it) with these additions:

- In French cookery **pralin** is a preparation used for flavoring confections made by mixing almonds with browned sugar and vanilla, then allowing the mixture to cool and pulverizing it to a fine powder.
- Also in French cookery, **praliné** is a small cake with an icing of butter cream flavored with pralin.

prawn
A shellfish much like the *shrimp*, but somewhat larger. Prawns may be used in most dishes that call for shrimp, but they are especially dramatic served *au naturel* as an appetizer or in Japanese *tempura.*

pre–
A prefix that indicates something that goes before; *earlier* or *previous.*
In cookery, denoting that which is done before such as *premixing* before adding to a preparation.

precook
To cook partially or entirely in preparation for the next step, as of a recipe.

preheat
- To heat food before proceeding to the next step in a preparation.
- To heat a pan, oven, etc. before adding food.

preserve
- To process food so as to keep it from spoiling for a time such as by pickling, smoking, canning, or freezing.
- Sweetened cooked fruit that is served as a condiment or used in the preparation of confections.

pressed duck
A method of preparing duck that involves removing the legs and breast meat, then making a sauce of the juices pressed from the carcass in an apparatus especially for that purpose.

pressure cooker
A heavy pot sealed so as to allow fast cooking at temperatures above boiling.

pretzel

A type of hard, glazed biscuit rolled into a tubular shape, often formed into a loose knot or other figure, boiled in water, then baked and salted.

primavera

- Originally descriptive of a preparation in Italian cuisine in which fresh vegetables are prominently featured, notably, *pasta primavera*.
- Generally, any preparation that is comprised mainly of vegetables, whether fresh or frozen.

prime

Indicating the highest grade, especially of meat.

prix fixe

French—price fixed. A complete restaurant meal that is served at a set price regardless of what is selected.

produce

Foodstuffs, especially fresh fruit and vegetables.

proof

- The action of yeast dough during the times it rests between mixing and kneading.
- A measure of the relative strength of an alcoholic beverage. In the U.S. *proof* represents twice the percentage, so that 80° is 40% alcohol. Bottlers control the proof by adding or taking away distilled water.

prosciutto

A spicy aged ham made in Italy; sliced thin and served as part of an antipasto, with melon, or as a component of other dishes.

protein

A basic component of living cells that is comprised of chains of amino acids.

provençale

Descriptive of a number of preparations that contain garlic and often, tomato.

provolone

- A firm Italian cheese that is smoked before curing.
- Any similar cheese manufactured in the U.S.

prune
 A plum that has been dried in the sun or an oven.

pudding
 A dish made of a variety of ingredients, sweet or savory, and that may be cooked, baked, or steamed.
 Sweet puddings, such as our instant (or nearly instant) desserts are smooth milk flavored puddings that are cooked with cornstarch as the thickener. Other dessert puddings such as apple brown Betty, are rougher in texture.
 Most savory puddings are coarse in texture, although some such as Yorkshire are more like a bread.

puff pastry
 A light flaky pastry made rich by the butter incorporated into the folds of dough when they are rolled out.

pumpernickel
 A dark bread made from coarsely ground rye.

pumpkin
 A large, roundish, orange-colored gourd, used in the U.S. mainly for the making of pie and jack-o-lanterns. Pumpkin can be made into a delicious soup or purée and, in fact, substitutes well in most recipes that call for winter squash.

punch
 A beverage that is a blend of fruit juices, wine, or liquor often with soda or tea added.

 Tip: For a party punch, place a ring of colored water or punch ingredients that have been frozen in a tube mold in the center of the punch bowl. Mint leaves or edible flowers can be also frozen in the ring.

purée
 Food that has been reduced to a smooth paste, as *tomato purée*. Thickness of a purée should vary depending on its intended use; one that is to be used as an ingredient in another dish may be thin whereas those intended for an hors d'oeuvre or canapé tray need to be somewhat thicker in order to hold their shape.

quaff
To drink, especially in a hearty fashion. Also used to describe a drink that may be *quaffed*, as a glass of ale.

quahog
An edible clam indigenous to the east coast of North America.

quiche
A rich custard baked in a pastry shell, often with a variety of ingredients such as cheese, ham, chicken, asparagus, broccoli, or spinach.

A good quiche is a rare treat indeed and quite easy to make, but for some reason many cooks shy away from it as beyond their talents—those who do should know that as long as there is sufficient egg to bind the mixture, that care is taken to remove excess moisture from other ingredients so as not to upset that balance, and that the oven provides even heat throughout, they can't fail.

quick bread
Descriptive of bread made with leavening that does not require rising prior to baking.

quince
A tart fruit that is edible when cooked, used mainly in the making of jelly and marmalade.

quinine
A bitter alkaloid that is the main ingredient in **tonic** or *quinine water*.

rabbit

Whether because of it's designation as a rodent, the universal love of Bugs Bunny, or visions of a cute Easter bunny, we don't consume very much rabbit in this country. Young and tender, however, the meat is white, flavorful, and somewhat less fatty than poultry—but you don't really want to know that, do you?

rack

A rib cut of meat prepared for roasting.

The rack is often trimmed and slit so as to form it into a circle with the cut end of the rib bones pointed upward; tied and baked, it is called a *crown roast*.

radish

A variety of edible root that may be colored white, red, or black and that differs in shape from small and round about the size of a cherry to an elongated growth that looks like a carrot.

ragoût

A stew of meat, poultry, or seafood, well-seasoned, and that may be prepared with or without vegetables.

raisin

Dried grapes that are used in the making of confections, and to garnish certain meat and vegetable dishes.

ramekin

⚜ An individual tart, or a pastry filled with a soft cheese mixture.
⚜ A small earthenware baking dish.

ramen

Any of a variety of Japanese preparations comprised mainly of noodles and broth, often containing bits of meat, seafood, or vegetables.

ranchero

Food prepared with a *salsa* or Mexican sauce of tomatoes, onions, and (usually hot) peppers such as *Huevos Rancheros,* an omelet that may be stuffed or topped with a variety of ingredients and salsa.

rancid

Descriptive of food with an unpleasant taste caused by fat or oil that has deteriorated.

range

A stove with several burners that may be individually controlled. The first kitchen range was a bricked area near the fireplace with a top surface that could be heated. A metal version fired with coal was patented in the seventeenth century, but never caught on as cooking was faster over an open fire. An improved version fueled by coal or wood was perfected in the early nineteenth century, about which time a gas version was developed as well.

Gas stoves had their detractors, especially among those who were aware of their tendency to blow up. Not long after the margin of safety improved and gas stoves became common throughout the kitchens of Europe and America, the electric stove came into being, but it too had problems. For one thing, most houses in the early part of the twentieth century were not wired for electricity. In addition, poor thermostats made heat control chancy, a complaint voiced to this day to those who prefer gas for cooking.

rarebit

* It could be *Welsh rarebit*, an adulteration of *Welsh rabbit*, or so-named because it is a rare (or unique) bit of food, so call it what you will. One thing is generally agreed—it is a delicious, thick, rich cheese sauce made with cream or ale and seasoning served over toast, and a rare treat indeed.
* We have come across several recipes with *rarebit* in the name that all seem to have cheese and a hefty dose of Worcestershire Sauce in common.

rasher

A rather imprecise measure; either a thin slice of bacon or a serving of several slices. Your choice.

ratatouille

A delicious vegetable dish that is prepared in a variety of ways all of which call for sautéed eggplant and garlic cooked with a number of other vegetables and seasoning. The dish often includes tomatoes as well.

Ratatouille is equally well represented hot or cold, as a side dish or a light meal.

ravioli

A stuffed pasta that is cut into small squares or rounds, boiled, and served with tomato sauce or gravy and sprinkled with Parmesan cheese.

The name is said to derive from a term meaning 'a thing of little value' in recognition of the one-time practice of stuffing ravioli with the remains from the previous meal. Talk about hiding leftovers! Hardly of little value today, ravioli may be stuffed with cheese, spinach, veal, beef, poultry, or any mixture the cook finds appropriate. (Maybe they're still hiding leftovers!?)

redeye, redeye gravy

Gravy made from strong, black coffee and the juice and fat of cooked ham.

red meat

This one can be controversial, so we'll just give you the choices:
- Meat that is dark before cooking such as beef or mutton, as distinguished from veal or pork.
- Any meat from an animal that is not a fowl.
- Any meat from a land animal as distinguished from seafood.

red pepper

Any pepper that is red in color whether mild as the bell pepper hybrid or pimiento, or hot such as chili or cayenne.
One point to note: the red bell pepper in the market is not a ripened version of the green bell pepper; it is a hybrid variety.

reduce

In cookery, to simmer or boil, as a liquid, so as to decrease in volume and intensify the flavor.

reduction

Any sauce or liquid that has been thickened and strengthened by reducing.

red wine

Wine colored a characteristic red by fermentation with the skins which also contain the tannic acid that imparts to a red wine its distinctive dryness.
A wine aficionado will hardly find this description adequate, but it is offered in the hope of being informative, however brief.

refine

To purify or improve in some way.
Sugar is refined by removing the impurities or unwanted portion of its source such as of cane or beets.

refrigeration
The cooling or freezing of food to preserve it, or the enclosure and peripheral equipment required to keep food cool or frozen. Food that requires cooling should be kept as close to freezing as possible without actually reaching 32°F or 0°C. For more about frozen foods, see *freeze*.

relish
⊛ A well-seasoned preparation of marinated chopped vegetables or fruit.
⊛ A condiment or appetizer such as olives, vegetable strips, or pickles.

rend, render
To melt fat by heating; often to heat meat or fowl so that the melted fat can be easily separated.

rennet
A substance extracted from the stomach of certain animals or from plants that curdles milk. Rennet is used to curdle milk for the making of cheese.

repast
A light meal.

rest, resting
The time during which dough sits or *proofs* between mixing and kneading.

rhubarb
The long green or reddish stems of a large-leafed plant that are cooked and sweetened for making into jellies, jams, or pies to which they impart a distinctive tart flavor.

rice
⊛ A cereal grain that is a food staple throughout a large part of the world.
⊛ To press food such as cooked potato through a sieve-like device so as to make it into small granules similar to rice.

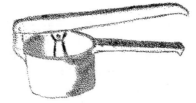

ricer
A device with a cantilevered handle that supports a pressure plate designed to force potatoes or other food through the holes of a perforated cup so as to *rice* or mash them.

ricotta
An Italian cheese, similar to **cottage cheese**, but somewhat drier even when fresh. Ricotta may be further dried or cured so that it is suitable for grating, but that type is seldom seen in the U.S.

Tip: Cottage cheese may successfully be substituted for ricotta in most recipes with only a slight variance in flavor if it is first hung in a tight wrapping of cheese cloth to release the excess moisture.

rigatoni
Large ribbed macaroni cut into short pieces.

rind
A sturdy outer covering, such as the skin of some fruit or cheese.

rinse
To cleanse lightly with water, but you knew that... or did you?
To rinse does not imply that food can be left to soak, or that warm water should be used, especially for vegetables—either will serve only to leech out vitamins, minerals, and ultimately, flavor. And it may not seem right to put 'dirty' lettuce, mushrooms, etc. in the refrigerator, but most foods will keep better if they are not rinsed until just prior to cooking or serving.

ripe
Descriptive of food that has matured fully or is ready to be eaten, such as fruit, vegetables, or cheese.

rise
To increase in size or puff up, as bread dough.

risotto
Italian rice cooked in broth or wine and flavored with Parmesan cheese.

roast
* To cook mainly by dry heat, as in an oven or near a hot fire or coals, such as a barbecue.
* A cut of meat that is suitable for roasting.

roasting pan
A pan with or without a cover that is used for roasting.
When covered, food in the roaster is at least partly braised by liquid in the pan.

rock candy
Large chunks of crystallized sugar made by allowing a strong concentration of sugar syrup to cool around a string.

Rock Cornish game hen
A small fowl that is a hybrid of the English Cornish hen and the American Plymouth Rock.

roe
The eggs of certain fish or shellfish.
Some roe are prized as delicacies such as those of the sturgeon that are sold as *caviar*, and those of the lobster or shad.

roll
* A small portion of bread, individually baked; often called a bun.
* A portion of food that is often filled, rolled into the shape of a cylinder such as a beef roll or *roulade*, or a jelly roll.

rolling pin
A cylindrical device, with or without handles, used mainly to roll out dough for pastry, pasta, etc.

Tip: Use a rolling pin to make bread crumbs—place the dried bread between two sheets of waxed paper and crush away!

rollmops
A fillet of marinated herring wrapped around a filling such as a small onion or gherkin and served as an hors d'oeuvre.

romaine
A type of lettuce with firm, oblong leaves.

Roquefort
A creamy, salty cheese made from ewe's milk. To be genuine, the cheese must be made from the milk of ewes raised in the district around Roquefort and cured in the caves of the area.

rosemary
A fragrant herb used extensively in marinades and in seasoning meat, fowl, and certain vegetables.

rose water
A liquid made fragrant by steeping rose petals in water. Rose water is used mainly in the making of confections.

roulade
A thin slice of meat spread with *forcemeat*, rolled, and braised or poached in a broth or sauce.

Back in the olden days, just a couple of decades ago, when the tough, lean cuts of meat were shunned, flank steak prepared in this way made not only a delicious meal, but a very inexpensive one. At the present market price, they are as likely to be made from round steak, veal, or pork.

roux
Butter and flour in approximately equal quantity that are blended and cooked slowly for several minutes to form the base for thickened sauces such as *béchamel*.

Tip: Roux-based sauces have a reputation for being loaded with calories, but they needn't be: instead of milk or cream, use a light vegetable or meat broth for the liquid, and make them thin so as to reduce the amount that adheres to the food they accompany—they will still provide ample flavor for the dish.

rum
A liquor distilled from molasses or sugar cane that has a particular affinity for fruit and thus appears mainly in sweet drinks with various combinations of fruit juices.

Even many who eschew alcoholic beverages find the distinctive flavor of run enticing in preparations ranging from meat marinades to confections.

rumaki
An hors d'oeuvre consisting of a piece of chicken liver and a slice of water chestnut wrapped in a bacon slice and broiled.

rutabaga
A root vegetable similar to the turnip, with yellow flesh that is usually boiled or baked; however, a judicious sprinkling of raw, thinly sliced or julienne cut mild rutabaga on salad is excellent.

rye
- The grain from a cereal grass used in the making of a variety of breads and in rye whiskey.
- Any of a variety of robust breads made from rye, such as *sour rye* or **pumpernickel** that are the breads most likely to be served with well-seasoned Germanic food.
- Rye whiskey, which is of only one type, that distilled from at least 51% rye grain in spite of the propensity in some parts of the country to describe any blended whiskey as *rye*.

safflower
The type of thistle whose seeds yield a light oil used for cooking or salad dressing.

saffron
The yellow-orange dried stamens of a type of crocus, used to flavor and color foodstuffs, especially sauces and rice dishes.

sage
An aromatic herb used to flavor sausage, marinades, and meats, especially chicken, pork, and veal.

sake, saki

A Japanese rice wine, served hot or chilled.

salad

The closest we can come to a definitive description is "a mixture of foods customarily served cold or at room temperature and usually with a dressing". Unfortunately that still precludes dishes such as hot potato salad... Oh, well.

To make matters worse, we can't seem to decide when to serve our salad—before the entrée, with it, after it, or in some cases, in place of it.

At one time, salads were strictly light affairs, made up of bits of greens and herbs delicately seasoned so as not to distract from the food they preceded or accompanied. For the most part, we tend to agree that the salad shouldn't outshine the main course. On the other hand, a salad of fruit, vegetables, meat, cheese, or seafood can serve to stave off hunger pangs while the main dish finishes cooking.

Unless tied to a routine considered inviolable in your household, try moving things around occasionally. We've had some fruit salads at the start of a meal that would have fared better served at the end of the meal with a bit of cheese. And don't miss an opportunity to suggest a light salad of greens or fruit to follow a fish course for cleansing the palate.

By the way, perhaps the hot potato salad that shouldn't be considered *salad* at all; maybe it's really a vegetable dish.

salad dressing

A seasoned mixture, sauce, or relish that garnishes a salad.

As an adjunct to the comments about **salad**, above, the dressing should also be considered. Heavy, flavorful concoctions are great in their place, but be careful not to dress a delicate green salad in a mixture that overwhelms it.

The presentation of a heavier salad of fruit, vegetables, meat, etc. will often be enhanced if the hearty dressing served with it is spread on the plate instead of over the mixture.

Salade Niçoise

A salad prepared by tossing shredded lettuce, peeled tomato wedges, and peeled cucumber chunks with a light dressing in a bowl that has been rubbed well with garlic, then arranging the mixture on a small plate with a variety of other ingredients such as black olives, anchovies, tuna fish, wedges of hard-cooked eggs, julienne slices of chicken breast, etc.

salami

Any of a variety of Italian cured sausages that are eaten hot or cold, often as part of an *antipasto*.

Salisbury steak

Ground beef mixed with onions, eggs, milk, and seasoning, then formed into a patty and fried or broiled.

Basically, Salisbury steak is a hamburger without the bun, promoted by a nineteenth century physician who believed that all food should be shredded before eating.

salmi

The meat of roasted wildfowl served in a rich wine sauce made in part from the pressed carcass and trimmings of the bird.

salmon

A large food fish with delicate (and delicious) pink flesh, often preserved by drying or smoking (*lox*), or poached and served hot or cold with a variety of sauces.

salsa

Spanish—sauce. A finely chopped combination of tomatoes, onions, peppers and spices customarily served with Mexican food. According to our dictionary the term is used mainly in the southwest, but anyone not aware of the growing popularity of Mexican-style fare needs to wake up and smell the tacos.

salt

Sodium chloride, a crystalline substance used extensively to season and preserve food.

Although salt is plentiful and inexpensive now, it was once prized as a necessity for curing meat and fish. We may attain some understanding of its value by recognizing that our word *salary* derives from the term for a salt allowance once paid to Roman soldiers.

saltimbocca
Italian—jump into the mouth. And this dish does! ***Prosciutto***, cheese, and sage wrapped in a veal scallop and sautéed in butter.

saltine
A thin, crisp cracker that has been sprinkled with salt.

salt mill
A utensil similar to a pepper mill used to grind coarse sea salt considered by some to be superior to common table salt.

salt pork
Fatty pork that has been preserved in salt.

sangria
Red or white wine mixed with fruit or fruit juice and sometimes fortified with brandy.
There are many versions of this beverage and our absolute favorite is the simplest. A very large, very ripe peach is sectioned and placed in a pitcher of red wine at the start of the meal. The wine is served throughout the meal, growing sweeter as the meal progresses; at the end of the meal the final glass of wine is served with the sections of peach.

sapsago
The American name for the Swiss *Schabziger*, a cheese colored green by its flavoring of powdered clover.

sardine
A food fish found along the coast of France and the Mediterranean. The sardine does not ship well and is known outside those areas where it is fished only as a cured delicacy. In the U.S., varieties of small fish, many unrelated to the sardine, packed in oil or other preservatives.

sarsaparilla
The roots of a tropical American plant used in the flavoring of soft drinks.

sashimi
A Japanese serving of slices of raw fish artfully presented. See also ***sushi***.

sauce

Generally, any liquid that is used to season food, from the simple juices left in the pan after cooking to those that may require hours of careful preparation such as a Sauce Españole.

In the U.S. we often equate *sauce* with something that is rich, exotic, loaded with calories, and too time-consuming to prepare for most meals, which is not necessarily true:

- Many sauces keep well in the freezer so that they can be made when there is time and brought out as needed for several meals thereafter.
- White sauce, or **béchamel** is a quick sauce that can be made with the liquid in which a vegetable has been cooked. The addition of seasoning or cheese will help to give life to otherwise bland vegetables.
- A similar sauce made from the juices of cooked meat with the fat removed or from broth is as easy as making pan gravy and, with the animal fat eliminated, is a lot healthier.
- Strictly speaking, salad dressings fall into this category as well. Try a **Sauce Vinaigrette** (below) made to your specifications for serving over cold meat, poultry, fish, or vegetables as well as salad.
- Most fruit can be cooked slowly and crushed to yield up a fine hot or cold sauce for dressing up ice cream or cake. Not as easy as opening a jar of sundae topping, but certainly more tasty and healthful.

saucepan

☀ Specifically, a deep, narrow pan with a rounded bottom and short handle, used to make and hold a sauce. The rounded bottom facilitates mixing and allows the pan to be placed in a bath of hot or cold water during preparation and serving. Mostly found in commercial kitchens, the short handle makes it possible to nest a number of pans side by side.

❄ Generally, used to describe any small- to medium-sized pan used for cooking on the stovetop.

Sauce Vinaigrette

Any of a variety of dressings made with oil and vinegar that can be served over virtually any cold savory dish in addition to salad. There are basically two types of Sauce Vinaigrette:

- Creamy style, made by forming an emulsion of the oil and vinegar. This is accomplished by thoroughly blending one to two tablespoons of vinegar with one tablespoon of oil. Once the emulsion has been established, additional vinegar or oil added in small quantities blends in easily. Flavor the dressing with herbs, spices, mustard, honey, minced vegetables, etc. Incidentally, if the emulsion fails, you will have made a clear dressing (below); just pretend that's what was intended all along and remember to shake before serving.
- Clear style, by far the easiest to make: put all of the ingredients in a jar and shake. The dressing will separate, so it has to be shaken lightly just before serving.

The type of dressing depends largely on taste and the food being served: *creamy* provides a stronger flavor because it tends to cling to the food; in addition to lighter flavor, *clear* imparts a gloss to the salad or meat it covers. Either dressing should be prepared ahead in order to allow the flavors to blend. And they both keep well in the refrigerator.

Tip: For vinegar, substitute left-over juice from your favorite pickles. Depending on the dish, dill or sweet works equally well.

Another Tip: Cultivate small jars of flavored vinegar or oil. Lemon zest in olive oil or tarragon in white vinegar for example, make great combinations.

sauerbraten

A German pot roast that is marinated for several days in a sweet and sour mixture of vinegar, sugar, and spices before cooking.

sauerkraut
Finely shredded cabbage that is fermented for several weeks in brine seasoned with juniper.

sausage
Finely ground and seasoned meat, packed into a casing.

The term is also used to apply to loose meat that has been similarly prepared.

Cured or cooked sausage such as frankfurters or bologna, often labeled *ready-to-eat* should be heated by boiling or steaming to bring out their flavor.

Fresh sausage or sausage meat that is perishable will only keep if it is refrigerated and should be fried or grilled.

Dry or summer sausage such as certain types of salami or pepperoni are usually eaten cold. Some of this type do not require refrigeration, but it's best to refrigerate all sausage just to be safe.

sauté

❋ To fry lightly over high heat. From the French, *to jump*, explained variously as to the (supposed) reaction of the food when it hits the hot pan, or of making the food jump by shaking the pan to keep the ingredients from sticking.

A sauté pan should have a thick base to hold heat well and shallow sides to facilitate turning or flipping the contents. To sauté properly, the pan should be quite hot so as to *surprise* the food and lock in the juices. Furthermore, the ingredients should not be crowded in the pan or steam will form and cook the food without browning and sealing it.

❋ A term used to describe a dish comprised of food that has been cut to pieces of approximately equal size and fried such as a *sauté of veal* or a *sauté of chicken*.

sauterne
A sweet white wine produced in the area of Sauternes, France or any wine purported to be similar.

savory
* An aromatic herb of the mint family.
* Descriptive of food that is not sweet.
* Often used to describe food that is flavorful or appetizing such as *a savory roast*.

scald
* To heat almost to boiling, such as milk.
* To cover food with boiling water so as to make it easier to peel; also called **blanching**.

scallion
A type of onion with a small white bulb and long, green, edible leaves. Scallions may be used whole as a garnish or chopped to add color and flavor, especially to salads and soups.

scallop
* A marine mollusk with a ribbed, fan-shaped shell, a prime ingredient in that prince of appetizers **Coquille St. Jacque**. Of the two types available, *bay scallops* and *sea scallops*, the bay scallops are smaller and more tender. Some recipes suggest that their delicate flavor be augmented with heartier seafood, but we disagree: nothing can compare with bay scallops that have been lightly cooked in butter and a touch of paprika.

* Originally, descriptive of creamed seafood served in a shell. Now a baked dish, usually of potatoes, layered with cream or cream sauce and topped with bread crumbs.
* A small piece of meat that is sliced and pounded very thin.

scaloppine, scaloppini
An Italian dish of thinly sliced and pounded meat that is sautéed and usually served with a light sauce.

scampi
* A shellfish similar to the shrimp, but somewhat larger.
* An Italian dish of shrimp or scampi that is sautéed in garlic and butter.

schnitzel
A German–Austrian preparation of veal cutlet that is coated with egg and breadcrumbs, then fried.

scone
A Scottish quick bread shaped somewhat like an English muffin that is baked on a griddle or in the oven.

scoop
Any of a variety of utensils used to measure or ladle, as a *sugar scoop* or *ice cream scoop*.

scorch
Now here is a term the cook doesn't want to hear, for it conjures up images of nasty smells and spoiled meals, but sooner or later we all have to deal with it.

There are only two hard and fast rules—get the pan off the heat and don't panic! The cook who turns off the heat and throws up his or her hands in despair is doomed. Often the damage is minor: if the food is quickly transferred to another pan while taking care not to include any overcooked particles, all may be well. Then do a taste test and hope for the best. There are lots of ideas for getting rid of that smoky taste; none are included here as they don't seem to work. If the food resembles a burnt offering, the only recourse is to quickly prepare a substitute or hope you remembered to stock up on frozen pizza.

scotch
An alcoholic beverage from Scotland characterized by the distinctive smoky flavor of the peat fires used to dry the barley malt from which it is distilled.

scrapple
A mixture of ground pork and cornmeal that is molded into a loaf, then sliced and fried.

seafood

A term used in cookery to characterize any edible creature that comes from the sea; usually depicting freshwater fish and crustaceans as well.

seasoning

- ✸ Generally denotes anything used to flavor food such as herbs, spices, and condiments, although purists will insist that it represents only the addition of salt.
- ✸ A procedure for tempering the surface of a pan.

  Most pans can be adequately seasoned by applying a light coat of oil and heating for about an hour on a very low burner or in a moderate oven. A well-seasoned pan will improve with age and perform almost as well as a nonsitck survace if rinsed with water, using a mild detergent only when necessary.

sec

French—dry. A designation of the property of certain wines, particularly Champagne.

secretion

A substance that is given off by or extracted from another.

seed

In cookery, the small nut-like ovule of certain plants used as food.

seed cake

A small cake or cookie that contains or is decorated with seeds such as sesame or caraway.

seltzer, selter water

- ✸ Specifically, a naturally effervescent spring water.
- ✸ In general use, water that is charged with carbon dioxide gas.
  Also called *carbonated water* or *club soda.*

Here we have two groups of purists: one group insists that the term applies only to water that is naturally effervescent while the other includes water that is carbonated just before serving. Neither would care for the carbonated stuff that is bottled in a factory and dispensed by the local grocery.

semi–
Latin—half. A prefix denoting *half* or *partial.*
In cookery, we use a variety of terms such as *semisoft, semisolid,* or *semisweet* that tend to be a bit ambiguous because everyone's taste and perception is not identical, but they are the best we can do to convey our impressions.

semolina
Coarsely milled durum wheat flour used in the making of pasta.

serrated
Of a knife blade that has small projecting teeth similar to those of a saw. A serrated blade is particularly good for cutting fresh bread as the teeth will bite into it without crushing the loaf. From time to time some enterprising entrepreneurs have tried to sell sets of such knives by demonstrating how easily they cut through a soft tomato. In our opinion, if a regular kitchen knife crushes a tomato, either the knife needs sharpening or the tomato is well past the time anyone should want to eat it.

sesame
The flat seed of an Asian plant used in cooking and for its oil.

shabu shabu
A kind of Japanese *fondue,* in which each diner selects and cooks various foodstuffs in water. To end the meal, the water which has become well-seasoned by the food cooked in it is served as soup.

shallot
A type of onion that tastes of a hint of garlic.

Tip: Shallots can be expensive and are not always readily available; a mild onion and a small amount of garlic will usually make a satisfactory substitute.

shandy, shandy gaff
A beverage of beer combined with lemonade, ginger ale, or ginger beer.

sharpener See *knife sharpener*

shave
To cut in the thinnest possible slices.

shears See *kitchen shears*

shepherd's pie
A meat pie baked with a covering of mashed potatoes. Traditionally, the meat is lamb, although now it is often ground beef.

sherbet, sherbert
A frozen dessert, generally made from fruit or fruit juice, sugar, and milk, whipped cream, egg white, or gelatin. See also, *sorbet.*

sherry
A Spanish wine fortified with brandy.

shirr
A method of cooking eggs by baking them in a *ramekin.*

shish kebab See *kebab*

shortbread
A kind of cookie made from a stiff dough of butter, flour, and sugar that is baked in a large sheet and cut into squares.

shortcake
A biscuit-like cake usually served with a topping of fruit and cream.

shortening
A fat such as vegetable shortening or butter used in baking to make pastry light and fluffy.

shoyu
Japanese-soy sauce.

shred
Depending on the preference of the shredder and the properties of the shredee, we may be talking thin strips or irregular pieces here.
Lettuce for salad can be shredded in long, thin, somewhat uniform strips on a *mandolin*, but there are those who would sooner make a Sauce Españole with bouillon—they will insist that lettuce should only be shredded by tearing it into pieces.

shrimp

A small crustacean prized for its firm meat which is similar to that of the lobster.

It is most likely that fresh shrimp will find their way to the table as hors d'oeuvre or garnish, but there is certainly no shortage of recipes for featuring them in main dishes as well.

Cooking shrimp. The way in which shrimp are prepared is important for, like most seafood, they become dry and tough when overcooked. Although many recipes call for cleaning shrimp and adding them to a dish raw, whenever possible we prefer to cook them independently, then allow just enough time in the preparation to warm them before serving. This allows better control of the cooking time, easier cleaning, and a chance for the cook to do some sampling in the process.

For **perfect boiled shrimp**, bring to a boil a pot of water or other liquid flavored with spices or vegetables that compliment the dish being prepared; add raw shrimp, cover the pot, and remove from heat; allow to stand for about fifteen minutes. That's all there is to it. The shrimp need only to be removed from the pot, then rinsed and cleaned, ready to be eaten or added to another preparation.

Tip: Strain the cooking liquid and save it (in the freezer if not for use immediately) as the base for a *court bouillon*.

shuck

⊛ A heavy outer husk such as that of corn.

⊛ The process of removing a husk or shell such as for corn or oysters.

sidecar

A cocktail made from brandy, orange liqueur, and lemon juice.

side dish

A term we use rather loosely to describe any dish that accompanies another, from the vegetables that complement meat or fish to the butter, sour cream, and chives served with a baked potato. A clever use of side dishes coupled with a borrowing from the customs of other cuisines can go a long way to dressing up a meal. A hearty vegetable dish for example, might be served before the main course instead of with it. Cooked fruit can be served with meat or poultry instead of the obligatory vegetables. Dare to be different—serve pine nuts or chopped egg to sprinkle over vegetables; or a light cheese sauce for the baked potato.

sieve

A utensil of finely woven mesh used to strain liquids, sift flour, or purée soft food; a strainer.

Tip: A sturdy sieve with a metal frame, especially one that has projections for holding it over a bowl makes a fine container for steaming food over boiling water.

sift

Basically, to put through a sieve, as flour, in order to separate out any large particles.

Recipes often recommend sifting before measuring in order to obtain a uniform volume. Even presifted flour settles with time and handling so that resifting is the only way to insure that the amount measured is correct for the recipe.

sifter

A sifter can be a sieve or strainer, or it can be a device with a wire blade that presses against the mesh and that can be rotated to force fine particles such as flour through it.

simple syrup

A liquid sugar used in the preparation of flavorings for beverages and in the certain confections; made by dissolving sugar in boiling water. The proportions, ranging from equal parts of sugar and water to about twice as much sugar as water, vary according to the use for which the syrup is intended.

siphon

- To draw off, as broth from a stock pot.
- A glass or metal container designed to hold carbonated water under pressure. Some siphons are equipped with a device for holding a capsule that injects the gas into plain water.

sirloin

- A section of meat that includes the fillet, sirloin, and rump steak.
- A large, usually thick steak cut from a sirloin of beef.

skillet

Essentially a frying pan although we frequently use the term to refer to a griddle as well.

skim

- To remove matter from the surface of a liquid, such as fat from gravy.
- To remove a readily accessible part, as butterfat from milk.

slaw See *cole slaw*

slice

To cut something into relatively uniform portions.

205

sloe, sloeberry

Either of two types of plum indigenous to North America, or a Eurasian plum also called *blackthorn* that is used mainly in flavoring jelly or liqueur.

sloe gin

Not a gin at all, but a liqueur made from the blackthorn plum. See *sloe*, above.

smelt

A variety of small, delicate, silvery food fish found in the cold waters of Europe and America.

smoke

To preserve meat or fish by exposure to smoke from a wood fire. The characteristics of the final product are dependent mainly on the pickling brine (if used) in which the food is soaked before smoking and on the type of wood used.

smorgasbord

Swedish—bread and butter table. A meal comprised of a number of dishes set out on a table or sideboard from which diners serve themselves.

snack

A small amount of food that is eaten as a light meal or between meals.

snap bean

A string bean with an edible pod; a green bean. See also, *beans*.

snifter

A rounded goblet narrowed at the top for serving brandy. We were delighted years ago to be the recipients of a set of fine, large snifters when a friend who was obviously not a brandy fancier marveled at the amount of brandy it would take to fill one! We explained that their purpose is capture the aroma of a small amount of brandy while the heat from one's hand warms the glass. Aficionados often look askance at the practice, however, preferring a narrow container that exposes less brandy to the air and thus imparts a lighter aroma for a longer period of time.

snow pea

A variety of the common pea with a softer pod that is edible when picked young; a common ingredient in Oriental cookery.

soap

We all know what soap is; this entry is just a sneaky way to make a couple of points about protection from harmful bacteria:

- Cleansing the hands and utensils after processing such foods as chicken requires soap or detergent; simple rinsing will not destroy bacteria.
- It is more important that wash water used for cleanup after a meal contain soap or detergent that is active, that is, will still make suds, than it is to have the water piping hot. Hot water will dissolve grease and make the task more pleasant, but only soap or detergent assures destruction of harmful germs and bacteria.

For added protection, do what the restaurants do: put a couple of tablespoons of chlorine bleach in the rinse water.

soave

A light, dry, white Italian table wine. From the Latin word for *delightful*, soave is just that.

soda

- ❀ The meaning of *soda*, the beverage, varies depending largely on where you live:
  - Carbonated water; also called *club soda, soda water,* or **seltzer**.
  - Commercially bottled, flavored carbonated water; also called *pop* or *soda pop*.
  - Carbonated water to which flavoring and sometimes ice cream have been added; also called a **phosphate**.
- ❀ Sodium carbonate; a white powder used in the manufacture of baking soda.

soda biscuit, soda cracker

A thin, usually crisp wafer made with baking soda.

soda water See *soda*

soft–boiled

Descriptive of an egg that has been boiled in the shell just long enough to set the white while only partially cooking the yolk.

soft–shell, soft shelled

Descriptive of **crab** that has recently shed its shell, before the new shell hardens.

sole

⊛ A type of European flatfish resembling the flounder and that is prized for its delicate white flesh.

⊛ In America, any of several varieties of flounder or of flatfish that resemble the flounder.

sommelier

The wine steward in a restaurant. It is the responsibility of the sommelier to know exactly what is contained in the wine cellar and to properly recommend and serve one that fits the diner's food, taste, and budget.

sorbet

A dessert of fruit or fruit juice and sugar that is frozen, but stirred periodically during the process so that the final product is the consistency of a purée.

sorghum

⊛ A type of millet cereal native to Africa used in the making of porridge and flat cakes.

⊛ A syrup much like molasses made from the sugar-rich stalk of the sorghum plant.

sorrel

A sharp-tasting green often used in salad; also call *dock*.

soubise

A purée of onions and rice used as a garnish in various meat dishes.

souchong

A variety of Chinese tea.

soufflé

- Puréed ingredients that are thickened with egg yolk and stiffly beaten egg whites, then baked.
- Often used to describe a dish that is light in texture similar to a soufflé.

soup

A liquid prepared from stock and other ingredients that may be strained (to remove all solids); puréed (to liquefy the solids); or served as it is cooked, with the solids intact.

Generally, soup may be classified as one of two types:

- **Clear soups** are essentially comprised of a broth or stock to which other ingredients have been added.
- **Thick soups** are those that have been made so by a purée, or by a *liaison* of roux, cooked rice, bread, or egg yolks and cream.

The legion of possible combinations for soup is far too extensive to be covered here, but we do have some suggestions:

- Keep your eyes open to possibilities: leftovers can make great soup or additions to soup, and they can be further disguised by mincing or puréeing.
- Try new combinations: a few pieces of chicken or fish might be an interesting addition to a vegetable soup based on beef broth. When in doubt, try a small amount of the combination first—no sense ruining a whole pot of soup with too much daring.
- Don't add root vegetables such as potatoes until the day the soup is to be served; even in the refrigerator they can sour a soup in a few days.

- Dress up an ordinary soup with an appropriate garnish just as you would a special one: a dab of sour cream or julienne strips of meat or vegetables for a clear soup; freshly chopped chives or basil for a creamed soup.

Tip: Unless the soup is to be a main course, keep it light. Serve only small portions of a very thick or rich soup so as not to distract from the rest of the meal.

sour cream

* Naturally soured cream that is used in baking; seldom seen these days because of pasteurization.
* Cream that is artificially soured; thick and smooth, it is used in cooking and as a condiment, such as for garnishing baked potato.

Can't seem to get by without mentioning the fake stuff that isn't sour cream at all. With less fat and calories, it may help to make you feel young and beautiful, but it certainly won't make you feel like you've eaten sour cream. Don't try it for cooking, because it breaks down when heated. On the other hand, it isn't too bad cold when mixed with other ingredients such as to extend mayonnaise or in the preparation of some desserts (see *grapes*) or dessert toppings.

sourdough

Fermented dough used as leaven for bread making.

In the days when commercial yeast was not so readily available, a sourdough starter was used and replenished after each successive baking. A starter might still be established naturally in a kitchen where much bread is baked and where yeast spores are likely to be lingering in the air, but in most modern kitchens they must be begun with yeast.

souvlaki

A Greek version of *shishkebab*.

soy, soy sauce

A dark, salty liquid condiment made from fermented soybeans; used extensively in Oriental cooking.

soybean

A nutritious legume that finds its way to the table in a variety of ways, from the familiar *soy sauce* and *soybean oil* to fillers in a variety of commercial preparations. *Tofu, miso,* and *tamari,* all derived from soybeans, have been a staple in Japanese cookery

for centuries and are rapidly becoming integrated into the American diet.
Low in fat and high in protein, soybean preparations are a healthful alternative to red meat.

spaetzle
Tiny dumplings from German cuisine made by forcing soft dough through a pastry bag or spaetzle machine into boiling water. Spaetzle is customarily served as a side dish, often with a robust gravy.

spaghetti
Long, thin strands of pasta; the name is derived from the Italian word for *string*. Spaghetti is often used generically to define a wide variety of similar pastas such as *angel hair*, *spaghettini*, or *vermicelli*.

spaghetti squash
A type of squash with meat in the form of spaghetti-like strands. Spaghetti squash can be baked or boiled without peeling, then cut open to extract the 'spaghetti' after the seeds and strings are removed. Serve with butter or a sauce in the same manner as flour-based pasta.

spaghettini
Italian—little spaghetti; or, carrying the etymology a step further (see *spaghetti*, above), *little string*. Long strands of pasta that are thinner than spaghetti.

spanakopita
A Greek pie of phyllo dough, filled with a mixture of seasoned spinach and cheese.

spatula
Any of a number of broad, flat kitchen tools of varying size and flexibility:

- **Cake or pastry spatula** - Much like a knife with straight sides and rounded end; ranging in size from three-quarters to one and one-half inches wide and four to nine inches long; generally comprising a flexible metal blade with wooden handle although smaller ones are frequently made from plastic or nylon.

Used mainly to spread icing, some spatulas have a serrated blade on one side that can be used to split a cake into thinner layers for filling.

If the spatula is to be used for such things as flipping *crêpes* or serving as well, a blade that is offset from the handle is most convenient.

- **Wooden spatula** – Available in a variety of shapes somewhat like flattened spoons, these rigid tools are mainly used for combining mixtures or stirring food as it cooks.
- **Scraper** – A flat piece of rubber, plastic or nylon one to two inches wide and about three inches long connected to a wood, nylon, or rubber handle.

Used mainly for blending or folding, a scraper is the perfect tool for cleaning the sides of a bowl or pan. Some are formed from a single piece of plastic or nylon; none are suitable for use with very hot ingredients.

- **Turner** – Generally the widest and sturdiest of all the spatulas, made from metal for use on a griddle or frying pan or of nylon for nonstick surfaces, with a handle that may be of wood or nylon.

The handle needs to be comfortable to grasp and offset sufficiently from the blade so that the implement can be easily controlled and not restricted by the sides of a pan. Flexibility of the blade depends entirely on how it is to be used: flexible for manipulating small, light pieces of food such as meat patties; very rigid for heavier duty such as placing hot dishes in an oven or broiler.

spear
A stalk, such as of asparagus.

spearmint
A plant of the mint family that yields an aromatic oil used for flavoring.

spice See *herbs and spices*

spinach
A medium to dark green leafy vegetable that grows in bunches; eaten raw in salad or cooked as a vegetable.

In addition to being healthful, spinach can be flavorful. The best flavor comes from fresh spinach in a salad, but be sure to rinse well as it can be gritty. The best method is to swirl the leaves in a pan of cold water, but don't allow them to soak.

Spinach does not take kindly to overcooking: place the leaves in a pan with only the water that clings to them after washing and heat just long enough for the leaves to go limp. For those who dislike that bitter aftertaste, a little butter and garlic usually disguises it well.

Tip: For those who make deep-fried food from time to time: just before serving, cook a few leaves that have been rinsed and thoroughly dried briefly in the hot fat, then drain them well. The result is a delicious and unusual garnish.

split pea
A dried pea used in the making of soup or purée.

Although most recipes advise soaking, unlike other dried beans, split peas don't seem to require it. Cooking time of any dried bean will vary according to age, but split peas that are not tender in less than an hour of cooking aren't likely to get any better. Split pea soup can be made with a variety of ingredients such as carrots, onions or ham, but as with many other foods, we have found the simplest to be the best:

Rosemary's Split Pea Soup

Rinse the peas several times in a pan of cold water until the liquid poured off is no longer cloudy, discarding any that float. Add water to about twice the level of the peas, bring to a boil and simmer slowly, adding more water if necessary. Once the beans are tender, add salt and pepper to taste. If necessary, cook off excess water or add more and cook a little longer to get the consistency desired, keeping in mind that the soup will thicken as it cools.

sponge cake

A very light cake of flour, sugar, and eggs that does not use leavening, but relies on trapping steam in the tightly bound batter as it bakes. Flavors used may vary and some cooks give the batter a little boost with baking powder.

spritzer

A beverage of wine and carbonated water.

sprout

❧ A tiny growth from a newly sprouted seed; a **bean sprout**.
Until a few years ago, only health food faddists were familiar with any sprouts other than those of the mung bean that make a regular appearance in Chinese food. Today most markets carry several varieties including delicate alfalfa sprouts and those of the radish that will spice up any salad.
❧ **Brussels sprouts**

spumoni

An Italian confection made up of layers of multi-colored and flavored ice cream and whipped cream.

squash

Any of various plants of the gourd family with a hard outer shell and fleshy meat that is edible when cooked.

stainless see *cookware*

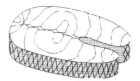

steak
- ❈ A piece of prime meat or fish, generally cut thick and across the grain.
- ❈ Meat that is cut or formed somewhat in the fashion of a steak.

steak au poivre
Steak that is rubbed with coarsely ground pepper several hours before cooking.

Steak Diane
Thin slices of steak prepared at the table with a variety of condiments and flambéed.

Steak Tartare
An appetizer of raw ground steak mixed with egg and garnished with onion, anchovy, and capers.

The dish without the garnish is said to have originated with the Tartars of Russia who shredded tough meat to make it more palatable. The French added the name and the garnish.

After shredded beef was first introduced into Germany by the Tartars it found its way into a number of other dishes common to Germany and the Western world, notably Salisbury steak and the cooked beef patty from Hamburg.

steam
The hot vapor produced by boiling water, often used to cook food. A few items that may be of interest:
- Steamed food retains more vitamins and minerals than food that is boiled or fried.
- Steaming food is easy. As long as there is water in the pan, the food is very forgiving—it may overcook, but it will seldom be destroyed in the process.
- Steam is **hot**. We all know that, but we tend to forget it as the vapor rising from food that is cooking quickly dissipates and cools in the air. Cooking with a steamer is a different matter—the steam is concentrated and can inflict a nasty burn, so be careful out there.

steamer
Any device or container used to steam foods:
- The *bamboo steamer*, a set of two or more nested bamboo trays with a lid. The tray bottoms are sturdy enough to hold a plate of food, but loosely woven to allow steam to

pass through and heat food.

 • **Nested pans** similar to a **_double boiler_** comprising a set of two or more pans with handles and a lid. The bottom pan is an ordinary saucepan; the upper pan or pans have perforated bases to allow the passage of steam.

• The **steamer insert** may be a pan with perforations in the base that nests over another pan or one with perforations all around that fits down into another pan. In either case, there should be stair-stepped ridges above the perforated area to allow the insert to fit pans of differing sizes.

• The **steamer basket** is a sort of perforated tray that is set into a pan and will expand to fit the pan, held off the bottom on three or four small legs.

Be sure that any steamer has a tight-fitting lid to trap the steam.

steaming mold

A container with a sealed lid and vent, used for steaming English puddings.

steep

To soak solid food in a liquid so as to tenderize, cure, flavor, or extract from the solid.

stein

A drinking vessel, especially one for holding beer.

stew

❉ To cook by simmering slowly in a liquid.

❉ A kind of soup made with a combination of fish, meat, poultry, or vegetables.

A stew may be based on a thick or thin broth and here the line between soup and stew is thinly drawn, except that a stew is generally heartier than soup and more likely to be served as a main course with the principle ingredients cut larger and less uniformly than they would be for soup.

stinger

A cocktail made from crème de menthe and brandy.

stir See **_beat_**

stir-fry

A technique borrowed from Oriental cookery that involves frying food quickly in a small amount of oil over high heat while constantly stirring. Stir-frying can be accomplished successfully in a frying pan, but the *wok* has the advantage of exposing less surface to the heat source and requiring less oil.

stock

A strained liquid in which meat, poultry, fish, or vegetables have been cooked; used as the base or flavoring for a variety of soups, stews, and sauces.

The ingredients for stock are often food that would otherwise be discarded such as bones and trimmings; as distasteful as it may sound to toss chicken or fish bones, overripe (not rotten) vegetables, or the peels and ends from a tomato or onion in the pot, they are quite flavorful and, remember, they will be strained out. The more common stocks are:

- **Brown stock** made from beef, veal, or poultry and vegetables that have been first browned in oil, and seasoning. Trimmings are not necessarily browned.
- **Fish stock** made from the bones and trimmings from fish, vegetables, and seasoning.
- **Vegetable stock** made mainly from chopped onions, carrots, and celery that have been browned in oil and seasoned. The intensity of this stock depends largely on the intensity of the browning.

Stock should be seasoned with salt and pepper to bring out the natural flavors of the ingredients and further flavored with herbs and spices, but don't get carried away: the dish that the stock ultimately embellishes will determine the final flavoring.

stockpot

A large pot used for making *stock*.

The stockpot in a commercial kitchen often simmers lightly on a back burner and collects the residue from food preparation that is appropriate to the type of stock.

Although not suited to most home kitchens, it may be a worthwhile to consider setting out a stockpot when entertaining a number of guests for whom a large amount of food is being prepared. If the stock turns out well, freeze it; if not, nothing is lost by throwing it away.

stollen
A rich German bread made by incorporating candied fruit and nuts into the bread dough.

stone-ground
Descriptive of grain that is crushed between stones, considered to be more flavorful and nutritious than that obtained by other methods.

stove See *range*

strainer
Often a *sieve* or *sifter* used to strain or filter sauces or other liquids, a strainer may also be an implement comprised of a fine mesh with a device for forcing food through it such as a *chinois* or *China cap*.

strawberry
A small fruit about the size of a cherry, irregular in shape with an outer layer of red meat that gives way to white inside.

straw potatoes
Deep-fried potatoes that have been cut into very thin strips.

string bean
A *green bean*, so-named for the fibrous string that runs the length of the pod.

stroganoff See *Beef Stroganoff*

strudel
A German pastry made up of layers of thin dough with a filling of fruit, nuts, or cheese.

sturgeon
Any of a variety of fresh- or salt-water food fish prized for their *roe* or *caviar*.

sub sandwich, submarine sandwich
Yep, you guessed it—the ubiquitous *sub* is short for *submarine sandwich,* named for its shape which is similar to that of a World War II submarine.

succotash
A vegetable dish of seasoned corn and lima beans.

suet
A type of fat from the layered tissue around the kidneys of sheep and cattle, used in cooking to lighten the texture of pastries.
See also, *lard*.

sugar
In cookery, a sweetener in dry crystalline or powdered form that is obtained mainly from sugar cane or sugar beets.
Liquid sugar or *simple syrup* used in the preparation of beverages and confections is made by dissolving sugar in water.

Tip: Flavored sugars, other than cinnamon and sugar, are not common in American kitchens, but it is quite easy to make up a variety that can be used for sprinkling over toast, pancakes, cake, and the like. Simply combine sugar with finely-ground flavorings such as anise, candied ginger, or candied orange peel.

sugar beet
A type of beet cultivated as a source of sugar.

sugar cane
A tall woody reed cultivated as a source of sugar.

sugar maple
A North American tree cultivated for its sap which is made into maple syrup and maple sugar.

sugarplum
A confection, often a piece of fruit, coated with sugar or sugar syrup.

sugar syrup See *simple syrup*

sukiyaki

A Japanese dish comprised of very thin slices of beef and a variety of vegetables cooked in a mixture of *sake*, *soy sauce*, sugar, and water.

As the success of this dish relies mainly on the tenderness of the slices of beef, here are a couple of suggestions that may be useful in other instances as well:

- When attempting to slice meat very thin (if you can't get the butcher to do it), place it in the freezer just long enough for it to get firm. A large piece may require repeating this process several times as the slicing nears the softer center that has not firmed up by chilling.
- Steep the thinly-sliced beef in water overnight to tenderize it, then use the liquid in cooking.

summer sausage

Dry sausage; so-called because it keeps well through the summer without refrigeration.

sun cured

Descriptive of food that has been preserved by drying in the sun.

sundae

A dessert of ice cream with a topping of syrup, nuts, whipped cream, etc.

The sundae was reputedly created and named when local blue laws prohibited the serving of ice cream sodas on Sunday.

superfine

Descriptive of sugar ground to an extremely fine powder, used in the making of pastry and confections.

supper

Here's another word with regional connotations; where you live probably dictates what it means:

- A light evening meal when the midday meal is considered dinner.
- Any evening meal, whether or not it is light, or whether the midday meal is called lunch or dinner.
- A light, late meal, often part of a social gathering.

sushi

A Japanese preparation of raw fish or vegetables that are rolled in cooked rice and wrapped in seaweed. The rolls are then cut into smaller bite-size pieces. See also, *sashimi*.

Swedish meat balls

Small balls of finely ground seasoned meat, bread crumbs, milk, and egg that are sautéed and served in a sauce made from the pan juices combined with cream.

sweet-and-sour

Descriptive of a dish, often of meat, that combines the flavor of sugar or honey with vinegar.

sweetbread

The pancreas of a young animal, usually calf or lamb, that is used as a garnish, in combination with other ingredients, or served alone.

sweetmeat

A confection such as candy or candied fruit.

sweet pepper

Any pepper that is not hot to the taste, especially a large, mild pepper shaped somewhat like a bell that may be green, yellow or red in color. See also, *green pepper*.

sweet potato

A tuber grown in the U.S., generally orange in color.
'Generally orange' because there are northern types that range from orange to white and are best cooked by baking. The southern types are more amenable to moist cooking. Usually served as a vegetable, the sweet potato frequently finds its way into dessert pie or pudding as well.
In this country the sweet potato is frequently called a *yam,* although the true yam, cultivated in Central America and parts of Africa, is huge by comparison.

sweet roll

An individual portion of bread baked from a sweet yeast dough that is embellished with fruit, nuts, icing, etc.

swine
A pig or hog.

Swiss chard
A type of beet with large leaves that are served as a vegetable.

Swiss cheese
* Any of a number of cheeses that are made in Switzerland, such as Emmentaler or Gruyère.
* An American-made cheese with a firm texture and characteristic air holes that emulate the Swiss Emmentaler.
Although often of good character, the standards for this cheese are so loosely defined that flavor ranges from bland to very sharp and consistency may only be assured by identifying a brand that is pleasing and unchanging.

syllabub
A beverage of milk or cream and sugar laced with fortified wine or brandy.

syrup
* A thick viscous liquid of sugar dissolved in water and often flavored.
* Fruit juice that has been boiled and thickened with sugar.

Tabasco®, tabasco pepper

Tabasco® is the trademark for a spicy condiment made from tabasco peppers.

table d'hôte

French—table of the host.

- ❀ A restaurant meal offering a limited number of choices; often at a set price, in which case it is called **prix fixe**.
- ❀ Descriptive of communal dining, especially at a small inn, where guests serve themselves from a buffet or large dishes of food passed among them.

table wine

A wine considered acceptable for serving with a meal in contrast to a fortified wine that is served before or after, or an inferior wine that is used in cooking.

By the way, don't confuse 'inferior wine' with that nasty stuff sold as 'cooking wine' that is better discarded and barely worth the price of the bottle that holds it.

taco

A small tortilla, folded and deep fried to make a hard shell that is filled with a variety of ingredients such as seasoned ground meat, refried beans, lettuce, tomato, cheese, etc. An American adaptation of a Mexican preparation.

taffy

A candy made from sugar syrup that is worked until cool and then pulled repeatedly until it achieves its characteristic gloss and texture.

tahini

A thick mixture similar to peanut butter that is made from sesame seeds.

Widely used in Middle Eastern cookery, tahini also makes an excellent dip for crackers, bits of pita bread, or vegetables when thinned with a little olive oil and flavored with garlic and spices.

tamale

A Mexican preparation that is made by spreading a cornmeal paste over softened corn husks or banana leaves, wrapping them around a filling of beef, chicken, or cheese, then steaming the rolls until they are firm enough to pull away from the leaves.

tamari

A type of *soy sauce*.

tang See *cutlery*

tangelo pomelo

A type of grapefruit that has been crossbred with a tangerine.

tangerine

A sweet, loose-skinned fruit akin to the orange; a type of mandarin orange.

The tangerine may be used in cooked dishes, but it is unquestionably at its best raw, often as a garnish to complement other foods.

tankard

A drinking vessel, oftentimes ornately decorated, with a handle and frequently, a cover.

tapioca

Starch obtained from the cassava plant used as a thickening agent and in the making of pudding.

tarragon

An aromatic herb with a flavor somewhat reminiscent of anise.

Tarragon is an excellent addition to green salad, either directly or by way of a dressing made from vinegar in which tarragon has been steeped; it also adds an interesting touch to light sauces.

tart

- A pastry comprising a filling of fruit, jam, etc. enclosed in a light crust.
- A type of small pie, usually round, with a light crust on the bottom and sides, filled with fruit, custard, or other sweet mixture for dessert, or with a savory mixture for an appetizer, brunch, or part of a light supper.

tartar See **cream of tartar**

tartare See *Steak Tartare*

tea
A beverage made from an infusion of dried leaves, fruit, spices, etc. steeped in hot water to extract their flavor.

tea ball
A small ball of perforated metal used to hold tea leaves, etc. that are to be steeped in water; an infuser.

teacake
A small cookie or pastry served with tea.

tea cozy
A padded cover placed over a teapot to keep it warm.

teakettle
A covered metal vessel with a pouring spout used for heating water.

teapot
A covered container, often decorated ceramic, with a pouring spout; used for brewing tea.

tempeh
A protein-rich, cheese-like food made from partially cooked and fermented soybeans, often used as a meat substitute.

tempura
A Japanese preparation of food such as shrimp or prawns, fish, and vegetables deep-fried in a delicate batter.

tenderize
To make tender, especially meat, as by marinating in a liquid or by pounding.

tequila
An alcoholic beverage distilled from the fermented juice of the agave plant.

teriyaki

A Japanese preparation of beef, chicken, or shrimp that is marinated in a special sauce and grilled.

terrine

- ❋ An earthenware container in which meat or fish is baked.
- ❋ A preparation of meat or fish baked in a pan lined with slices of bacon.

Tetrazzini

Descriptive of a dish made with chicken or turkey, pasta, mushrooms and white sauce.

Tex–Mex

Designating the Americanization (or Texanization) of Mexican foods; American cuisine with a strong Mexican influence.

thermometer

A device for measuring temperature, several types of which are useful to the cook:

- A general-purpose food thermometer is comprised of a thin metal tube about six inches long with a circular dial at the end that measures a full range of temperatures, from freezing to boiling; used to check ingredients when temperature is critical such as that of liquids when making yeast dough. Convenient, too, for making certain that food cooked in a microwave has heated through.
- A meat thermometer is similar to the general-purpose thermometer, but calibrated for higher temperatures with a larger dial for easy reading from outside the oven.

Tip: When testing meat, insert the probe as near to the center as possible, but be careful not to touch bone or the reading will be inaccurate.

- An oven thermometer is necessary only if there is reason to believe that the stove's thermostat is off or there are hot spots in the oven. It is unlikely that either can be corrected, but it may be possible to compensate for them.

- A refrigerator or freezer may also house a faulty thermostat or develop hot spots. A thermometer designed to measure cooling temperatures will confirm that the unit is maintaining the correct temperature; moving it around periodically will detect any unevenness throughout the unit.
- A deep-frying thermometer designed to hang from the side of a pan will insure that fat for cooking remains at the proper temperature.

thickener

Anything designed to give extra body to a liquid such as arrowroot, cornstarch, flour, or tapioca.

Kneaded butter (**beurre manié**) is a blend of approximately equal parts of flour and butter; six to eight tablespoons of each is enough to thicken about a quart of liquid.

If flour alone is to be added to hot liquid, blend it with water to a smooth paste to prevent lumps. See **arrowroot**, **cornstarch**, and **roux** for additional suggestions.

thyme

An aromatic herb with grayish-green leaves.

Thyme is a constant companion of **basil**; few recipes call for one without the other.

timbale

- A preparation of custard-like consistency baked in a timbale mold.
- A round, straight-sided, metal dish in which a timbale is cooked or served.
- A combination of food in a cream sauce, served in a pastry crust.

Toad-in-the-Hole

An English dish comprised of small sausages baked into a **Yorkshire pudding**.

toast

- To brown over a fire, under a broiler, or in a **toaster**, such as a slice of bread, bagel, or English muffin.
- To raise a glass and drink to the health of another.

The custom originated in a period when the well-mannered host was expected to raise a glass and drink first in order to prove to those in attendance that the wine they were being served had not been poisoned. Tough party!

toaster, toaster oven

Anyone out there who remembers when toasters didn't pop up? or, heaven forbid, when they were only a device that held bread over a burner on the stove? Changing styles have reflected alterations in lifestyle as well: from two-slice to four-slice for faster service; to toaster ovens, that precursor of the microwave; to wider slots to accommodate English muffins and bagels. Where will it all end?

toddy

A beverage made with whiskey, rum, brandy, or other liquor mixed with sugar, hot water, and spice, often a cinnamon stick.
One of the best reasons for living in a cold climate!

toffee

A hard candy made from sugar, cream, and butter, flavored with vanilla or rum.

tofu

A soft textured soybean cheese used extensively in Oriental cookery, often added to soups and **stir-fry**.
Tofu is rich in protein and makes a good substitute for meat. It can be cubed and added to most soups without altering the flavor; in fact, tofu tends to take on the flavors that surround it.
Tofu sticks, kind of like fish sticks, are made by cutting one-quarter inch slices of tofu into rectangles about one inch by two inches, coating them with seasoned nutritional yeast, and frying them slowly until firm.

Tip: Anyone fond of egg salad who is trying to cut down on eggs would do well to crumble tofu, mix it with mayonnaise, and season to taste. The resemblance is amazing.

Tofu keeps well in the refrigerator sealed its original package or, once the package has been opened, in a lidded dish covered with fresh water. It can also be frozen in the original package.
Once frozen and defrosted, the texture becomes somewhat firmer and spongy, similar to that of cooked chicken. Before using, gently squeeze out any excess moisture that the tofu has absorbed. Tofu that has been frozen should be seasoned much more lightly than fresh as it soaks up flavor and sauces like a sponge.

Tokay
A variety of grapes native to Hungary or wine that is made from those grapes.

tomatillo
A green tomato-like vegetable from Mexico.

tomato
The red or yellow fruit of a plant of South American origin.
Once suspect as a member of the poisonous nightshade family, tomatoes have become a mainstay in salads, soups, a wide variety of condiments, sauces, and other preparations.

Tip: Thin vegetable soups and some cold sauces fairly cry out for the seeds and juice from the tomato, but the seeds can be bitter and the liquid inside detrimental to some sauces or other preparations.
To remove the bulk of the seeds and excess liquid, simply cut off the top of the tomato and squeeze gently; if necessary, scrape with a small knife.

Another Tip: Raw tomato is inclined to shed its moisture and adversely effect certain other foods, especially cheese, therefore, it is best to add raw tomato to a sandwich or salad just before serving.

Baked or fried tomato Clean a tomato as outlined above, lightly salt the insides and invert on a rack to drain for about thirty minutes. Fill the tomato with bread stuffing, puréed vegetables, etc. and bake for about thirty minutes in a moderate oven. A neat way to use up extra stuffing or vegetables and create a dressy dinner plate at the same time.
Especially good at breakfast or with meat is a thick slice of the drained tomato (without stuffing) that has been fried lightly in the pan after eggs or meat are done.

tomato paste
A thick purée of tomatoes that have been reduced by long, slow cooking to intensify their flavor.
Tomato paste is used in small amounts for flavoring, such as in sauces or soups.

tomato purée
Puréed tomatoes that have been cooked to reduce them, but not so long as for *tomato paste*.
Tomato purée is used for flavoring or as a base for sauces.

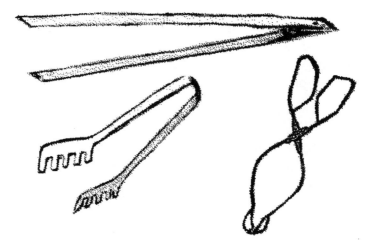

tongs

Any of a variety of grasping tools used in cooking and serving.
Wooden tongs such as those pictured at the top of the page are probably the most versatile: use them to turn food in a frying pan, pluck vegetables out of boiling water, even to stir the pot, and for one of the most difficult tasks in the kitchen... pulling out a single piece of pasta to test for doneness.
Metal tongs can do all of those tasks as well, but if care is not taken, they will scratch pans.
There are tongs designed specifically for serving cutlets, spaghetti, and the like, but even here the wooden ones work as well.
Heavy duty tools such as the tongs on the lower right are designed more for lifting custard cups, small pots, or canning jars from boiling water.

tonic, tonic water

A carbonated beverage flavored with *quinine*; quinine water.

torpedo

In some parts of the country, a type of large sandwich of meat, cheese, etc. served on a long roll with lettuce, tomato and a variety of other condiments.

tortellini

Small rounds of pasta that are stuffed with meat or cheese, then folded over and fashioned into little rings.

tortilla
A type of Mexican flatbread made from unleavened corn meal or wheat flour and fried on a griddle.

The soft tortilla is often used like a spoon of bread to scoop up food or rolled around a variety of ingredients and baked in a sauce, although some preparations, such as the tostada call for deep fat frying to make them crisp.

Tip: Tortilla fillings don't have to be Mexican—for a change of pace, wrap them around egg or tuna salad, chopped vegetables with a thick dressing, or even a hot dog!

tostada
A small tortilla that is fried crisp and topped with a variety of ingredients such as meat, refried beans, salsa, lettuce, tomato, sour cream, etc.

tournedos
Small slices or steaks cut from the heart of the *fillet* of beef, generally grilled or sautéed and served in a variety of ways with an elegant sauce or garnish.

trattoria
In Italy, a restaurant or tavern that serves simple food and drink; in the U.S., a modest name for a restaurant that often belies the elegance of the food and drink served within.

treacle
British—molasses. In the U.S., a molasses candy.

trencher
A board or platter on which food is carved for serving.

In the Middle Ages, when individual plates were uncommon, a thick slab of bread called a *trencher* was set at each place to hold food and catch the drippings.

It is unclear whether the term **trencherman**, used to describe one who eats heartily, is meant to characterize a person likely to eat from the serving platter or one who eats everything including platter!

tripe
The stomach lining of cattle, pigs, or sheep that is used as food. It is not surprising that the word *tripe* is also used to describe a

thing of little value, for tripe (the food) is bland, difficult to digest, and nutritionally insignificant. There are those, however, who consider tripe a delicacy, attracted no doubt by the elaborate preparation required to make it palatable.

trivet

A footed metal stand, often decorative if used to hold a heated dish off the tabletop, or funtionally plain if holding food above the water in a steamer pan.

The trivet originally held a cooking pot above the fireplace hearth.

truffle

- Any of a variety of edible fungi that grow beneath the ground near or on the roots of trees and that are harvested with the aid of pigs or trained dogs. Truffles are highly prized, scarce, and therefore very expensive; mainly used sparingly in sauces and pâtés.
- A delicate chocolate confection variously flavored with liqueur, spice, nuts, etc.

truss

To bind the wings and legs of a fowl before cooking.

try

To melt or render fat, as to remove impurities.

tube pan

A deep round baking pan with a hollow tube in the center.

The tube pan is generally used for baking a light cake such as angel food that requires even baking throughout.

Tip: Use a tube pan for preparing a meat loaf, savory mousse, or molded dessert. Serve the unmolded food with a side dish or garnish in the center for a dramatic presentation.

tuber

A swollen root stem, such as the potato, that is edible.

tuna, tunny

Any of a number of large saltwater game or food fish, or related fish such as the bonito. One look at the space on a grocery shelf devoted to canned tuna will attest to its popularity.

Normally relegated to that of a quick lunch straight from the can or mixed with mayonnaise for a sandwich, tuna can be served in a variety of other ways:

- Plain or mixed with dressing and minced celery to make a filling for fresh tomato; served as an appetizer or a light lunch.
- Puréed with cream cheese, Neufchatel, or creamed cottage cheese and spiced with pickle relish or salsa and hot sauce to serve with crackers as an hors d'oeuvre.
- As a primary ingredient in a **Salade Nicoise**.
- Heated slowly in a frying pan and stirred (tuna in oil works best for this) until the consistency of a purée, then blended with a thin béchamel sauce, a light chicken broth, or Italian tomato sauce to be served over pasta.

And finally, anyone fond of fresh (or fresh frozen) fish will be pleased with the tuna steaks that are becoming more readily available in the market. Cooked lightly with a minimum of embellishment, they are considerably more elegant than canned tuna and a real treat.

turbot

A flatfish with delicate white flesh fished in European waters.

tureen

A broad, deep, covered dish used for serving soups and stews.

turkey

A large North American bird widely cultivated for food.

Once limited to the Thanksgiving or Christmas table, the turkey in recent years has taken on much greater importance along with chicken as a healthy alternative to fatty red meat. Whole birds are readily available in the market all year along with a proliferation of concoctions that substitute turkey for ground beef, **pastrami**, and sausage.

turmeric

A plant of India with a fleshy, aromatic root stock that is ground to powder and used as a spice. An essential spice in curry that gives it its characteristic yellow color.

turner

A *spatula* used to manipulate food on a cooking surface such as a fry pan, wok, or griddle.

turnip

A plant of the mustard family with a bulbous white or yellow root eaten as a vegetable.

turnover

A pastry made from a round or square of pastry dough that is filled, folded over, and baked.

Although we are more accustomed to sweet fillings such as fruit, jam, or a cheese concoction, a turnover may also be filled with meat or vegetables and served as a first course or made bite-sized for hors d'oeuvres.

urn
An often ornate vessel with a spigot used to warm and serve beverages.

utensil
Generally, any tool, implement, or container used in cookery.
In addition to the traditional assortment of pots and pans, cutlery, etc. new utensils appear on the market regularly, testimony to the American obsession with gadgets; however, even a diehard may be interested in some advice:

- Nothing in the Constitution stipulates that we must have all of the latest devices. Before buying, consider whether the item is redundant, that is, designed for a task that can be done with tools already available, and how often it is likely to be used. The avid collector with drawers full of debris may also want to consider whether the proper tool will even be found when it is needed.

- Don't get caught up in a fad. Before you buy that slicer, dicer, smoker, steamer, dryer, juicer that will make you the world's most efficient chef, consider first, as mentioned above, whether you are likely to use it. Then, if you are determined, check first to see if all the claims of improved health and fitness are justified. If you are not sure, wait a bit and look for ads selling the *wonder tool, as advertised on TV'* with the price slashed from $59.95 to $9.95.

- Avoid sets of things, especially of cookware and cutlery, for it is likely that any set will have to be supplemented in some way, and will usually contain at least one item you will never use, unless of course you feel that item might make a nice Christmas gift for a relative. For the price of an umpteen-piece set you can buy fewer pieces of superior quality.

- Get tools that suit you—pan sizes compatible with your style of cooking, tools with handles that fit your grip, etc. It's nice to have utensils that are artfully designed, but if they aren't functional all you have is an expensive paperweight.

- Buy the best you can afford, especially of the tools you use the most. And *best* is not necessarily *most expensive.*

vanilla
A liquid flavoring, extracted from the seed pod of the vanilla plant or manufactured artificially. Pure vanilla is somewhat more expensive than artificial, but is far superior for most uses.

vanilla bean
The long black seed pod of the vanilla plant that is used in flavoring confections.

veal
The delicate meat of calf.

vegetable
A plant cultivated for food.
Although meat is often considered the mainstay of our diet, most of us consume many more types of vegetables than we do meat. If we include all vegetation used for food including grain, nuts, fruit, and the like, it is apparent that food from plants constitutes the bulk of our intake.

vegetable brush
A brush used for cleaning vegetables.
Here's another plea for conserving the nutrition and flavor of food: whenever possible, use a soft brush or none at all when rinsing, but keep a stiff-bristled brush on hand for vegetables such as carrots and potatoes in lieu of peeling them.

vegetable oil
Cooking fat obtained from vegetables which because of their composition are generally considered healthier for general use than those obtained from animal fat.

velouté
A white sauce made from chicken, veal, or fish stock thickened with a *roux*. *Velouté* is the base for many white sauces.

vermicelli
Long strands of pasta that are thinner than *spaghettini*.
The name derives from the Italian word for *worm* or *little worm*, which seems a bit unfair, for *vermicelli* the pasta is longer and tastier than *verme* the worm.

Vichy, à la Vichy
A term often used to describe preparations that feature carrots.
The hot mineral springs of Vichy in France have long been considered favorable for easing conditions of the liver, and carrots thought to be similarly beneficial are very much a part of the diet there.
On the subject of more recent studies, *carotene* available in large quantities in carrots has received considerable credit as a cancer preventive ...and cooking seems beneficial as the carotene is much more easily absorbed.

Vichyssoise
Creamed potato and leek soup flavored with onions, usually served cold sprinkled with chopped chives.

vinaigrette
⚛ Descriptive of a preparation served with a mixture of oil and vinegar that may be seasoned and variously flavored.
⚛ *Sauce Vinaigrette.*

vinegar
An acidic liquid produced by fermentation of distilled alcohol, wine, apple juice, or malt; used as a condiment or preservative. Vinegar may be further flavored with herbs.

vintage

The classification of wine by district, vineyard, or the year in which it was produced, often an indication of the quality of the wine.

The laws for classifying wine vary from one nation to another. In France where wine making is regulated, if confusingly so, and where the vintners of a district are fiercely protective of their vintages, the name of the district may offer insight into the type of wine or grape; the vineyard is akin to a brand name on foods, and the year tells not only the age of the wine but allows one to pass judgment based on the quality of a harvest that varies from year to year.

German wines are more closely regulated, and with characteristic Teutonic precision are rated for quality based on three major classifications: ordinary table wine that is not normally exported, Qualitätswein b.a. or Q.b.a that only attests to origin in one of eleven regions of Germany, and Qualitätswein mit Prädikat that is a wine of distinctive quality. Qualitätswein mit Prädikat normally carries a more prestigious label indicating specifically where it was produced and the vintner's name as well. It is further divided into five categories that indicate for the most part the timing of the harvest.

In the U.S., most wine is produced in parts of California which do not suffer the severe changes in weather that can harm a vintage or produce a great one. As a result, we have been blessed with an ample supply of inexpensive wine of relatively consistent quality. Increasingly, however, small vintners are producing lines of vintage wine that compare favorably with the best that France has to offer.

vintner

❋ One engaged in the making of wine.
❋ A specific vineyard, similar to a brand name.

vodka

An alcoholic beverage distilled mainly from grain to 190 **proof** (95% alcohol) and cut with distilled water. U.S. vodka is by law 'without distinctive character, aroma, taste, or color' and therefore mixes well with almost anything. Imported vodka, on the other hand may contain flavorings such as pepper or caraway.

walnut

Generally, the English walnut, produced mainly in the U.S.; the seed of the walnut tree used as an addition to salads and in the making of confections. See also, *black walnut*.

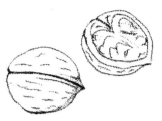

wasabi

Japanese horseradish.
Available as a ready-to-serve paste or a powder that is mixed with water, a small green mound of wasabi is served as a condiment with many Japanese dishes.

wassail, wassail cup

- A traditional Christmas drink of fortified wine, brandy, or ale flavored with apple and spices.
- A festive toast, as to ones health and good fortune.

water biscuit

A type of cracker made from flour and water.

water chestnut

The nut-like fruit of an aquatic plant, used extensively in Chinese cooking.

watercress

An aquatic plant of the mustard family used mainly as a garnish and in salads.

watermelon

- A large gourd-like fruit from a vine that has a hard, green outer shell and sweet, red edible meat impregnated with dark seeds.
- A hybrid with sweet golden flesh.

wax bean

A type of string bean with a yellow pod. See also *beans*.

Welsh rarebit, Welsh rabbit See *rarebit*

western omelet

A preparation of beaten eggs, ham, onions, and green peppers that is fried like an omelet.

Westphalian
A type of gourmet ham produced in the region of Westphalia in Germany.

wheat
Any of a variety of cereal grasses cultivated for their edible grain used in the making of flour for breads, pastries, and pasta.

wheat germ
The nutritious embryo of the wheat kernel that is usually separated before milling and sold as a cereal or food supplement.

whetstone
A sharpening stone.

whip
* To **beat** so as to induce air into a mixture in order to increase its volume and lighten its texture.
* A **whisk**.

whipping cream
Cream that contains at least 30% butterfat, suitable for beating to a thick consistency. See also **light whipping cream**, **heavy cream**.

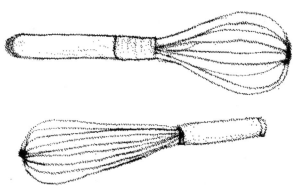

whisk
* A kitchen tool comprised of a set of wires bent into a bulbous curve with the ends wrapped or secured to a handle; also called a *wire whisk*. These whisks are available in a variety of sizes, shapes, and degrees of flexibility depending on the tasks for which they are intended.

* A device made up of a pair of meshed blades connected to a drive wheel that in turn has a handle connected to it; also called a *rotary whisk* or *egg beater*.

The necessity for using two hands, one to hold the device and the other to turn the handle, makes the operation rather awkward, especially if the drive wheel does not operate smoothly. With a little practice, the wire whisk is much more convenient and requires less effort for most jobs.

whiskey, whisky

An alcoholic beverage distilled from grain.

In America it's spelled *whiskey*; in Scotland (and among lovers of *Scot's whisky* everywhere) it's *whisky*.

white pepper

Peppercorns from which the dark hull has been removed; pepper ground from such peppercorns.

white sauce

A sauce made from milk, cream, or light chicken or veal stock, thickened with a *roux* of flour and butter. See also, *béchamel*.

white wine

Wine that is produced from the juice of the grape only, without any skins present during fermentation.

whiting

A north Atlantic food fish with fine white textured flesh.

whole-grain

* Descriptive of flour that has been made from the complete grain including the shell or *bran*, and the embryo or *germ*. Flour thus milled tends to be more coarsely ground than other bread flour.
* Descriptive of bread made from such flour or from white flour to which bran and germ have been reintroduced.

whole milk

Milk that has not had any butter fat removed.

whole wheat

Descriptive of flour milled with the bran and germ intact, or of bread made from such flour.

wiener

* A smoked sausage of pork or beef; a wienerwurst.
* A frankfurter.

Wiener Schnitzel

A breaded veal cutlet that may be sautéed or deep-fried.

wild rice

The dark, rice-like grain of a North American aquatic grass; usually served mixed with brown or white rice.

wine

* A beverage made from the fermented juice of grapes.
* A beverage from the fermented juice of any plant such as apples, berries, or dandelions.

Local custom or law may require that preparations not made from grapes be qualified by a descriptive name such as *apple wine* or *dandelion wine*, or they may be prohibited from being called wine at all.

wine cellar

A place for storing wine. Whether in a cabinet, a closet, or a cellar, the quality of wine is best preserved undisturbed at a constant temperature, preferably in the range of 50° to 60° F., in a moist and dark environment. Bottles should be stored on their side to insure that the cork does not dry out.

wine cooler

* A bucket or similar container, often ornate, for keeping a bottle of wine chilled prior to being served.
* A beverage of wine, fruit juice, and carbonated water.

winepress
A device used to press the juice from grapes.

winery
A place where wine is made or sold.

Winesap
A variety of tart apple with dark red skin.

wine steward See *sommelier*

wintergreen
An oil or flavoring derived from a type of North American ever-green shrub.

wok
A bowl-shaped Chinese cooking vessel with long, sloping sides that has gained considerable popularity in American kitchens. The wok has several advantages over conventional European cookware for certain types of cooking:
  • The small area in contact with the heat source allows frying with less fat.

- The thin metal sides provide space for foods to retain their heat without further cooking while other foods are being cooked.
- The gradual slop of the sides makes it an excellent base for a **bamboo steamer** of any size.
- The rounded bottom and sloping sides facilitate the task of finishing off a simple sauce using the pan juices without removing food from the pan.
- The small base requires less oil for deep fat frying while the wide top reduces spatters. In addition, many woks are fitted with a wire tray that attaches to one side for draining food.
- One final trick we discovered: Some woks come with a ring that provides a base for them off the heat. If the base fits around a stove top burner it can be used to raise the wok above the heat source for slow warming of foods.

As versatile as the wok is, it does have limitations: the thin metal is a poor conductor of heat, so that food cooked in it requires constant attention; and the small cooking surface is not suited to preparing large quantities of food at one time.

Worcestershire

A commercial sauce prepared from vinegar, molasses, anchovies, and a variety of spices.

wurst

Sausage; often modified to indicate a particular kind of sausage such as *bratwurst, knackwurst,* or *liverwurst*

yakitori
A Japanese preparation of small pieces of chicken that are marinated in a sweet, dark sauce and broiled.

yam
Commonly, in the U.S., a sweet potato. The true yam, however, cultivated in parts of Central America and Africa, is considerably larger and not nearly as nutritious.

yeast
- A leavening for bread or pastry dough available in powdered or cake form.
- A food supplement made from the inactive yeast that remains after brewing beer, available as a powder or flakes; also called nutritional yeast or *brewer's yeast*.

yogurt
A custard-like dairy product made from milk soured with a bacteria culture and allowed to ripen for twelve to twenty-four hours.
Yogurt that contains active cultures is the most nutritious as these cultures are a significant aid to digestion; any product containing them will say so on the label.
Starter culture is available in most health food stores along with instructions for making yogurt at home; fresh home-made yogurt is easy to make, not nearly as acidic as the commercial variety, and much better tasting.

Yorkshire pudding
An English quickbread of flour, milk, and eggs, often baked in the same pan as the beef with which it is to be served so as to soak up the juices. See also, *Toad-in-the-Hole*.

zabaglione

An Italian dessert consisting of egg yolk, sugar, wine, and flavoring made light and thick by constant whisking over heat.
Zabaglione may be served alone or as a topping for pudding, ice cream, or fruit.

zest

The skin of an orange, lemon, or grapefruit with the white rind removed.
It may seem an arduous task to peel the fruit with such care, but it becomes easier with practice and well worth the effort for the essential oils are contained in the thin outer skin and the white does nothing but add bitterness.

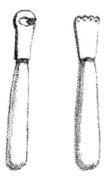

zester

A utensil designed for cutting thin strips of zest from citrus fruit, either to decorate them or for the zest itself.
A zester, especially the one on the left with a single blade, can be used to cut decorative *flutes* in fruit or vegetables as well. The knife on the right that has four or five smaller blades is ideal for cutting strips of zest or vegetables, such as from carrots or beets, that can be used to decorate salads or other dishes.

zucchini

A type of squash that looks like a cucumber with dark green skin.
Zucchini is eaten raw sliced in a salad or as a garnish, and cooked, as in a *ratatouille* or as zucchini boats—halves of zucchini hollowed out and steamed or baked with a filling of seasoned vegetables or ground meat.

zwieback

Bread that has been sliced, then dried and browned in an oven.

And finally...

Some of Our Favorite Food Tips that Didn't Fit in Anywhere Else
(as well as those that bear repeating)

Baking and Roasting:

- Popovers, soufflés, and quick breads will rise best if placed on a low rack in the over. Racks overhead should be removed to prevent the food from rising into them.

- When baking several dishes at the same time, stagger them on the shelves in the oven to allow the air to circulate and bake them all evenly.

- To substitute a square cake pan for a round one, keep in mind that a square pan holds about a third more ingredients than a round one of the same size.

- Test a cake or custard to determine if it is done by inserting a toothpick or wooden skewer near the center; if it comes out dry, the pan is ready to remove from the oven.
  We have heard of using a strand of spaghetti for testing, and it works; just be careful that it doesn't break off inside or, if it does, remember to remove it before serving.

- After removing custard or custard-like dishes such as quiche or lasagna from the oven, allow them to rest for a few minutes before serving, giving the custard time to set.

- Carefully follow recipe directions for cooling cake, bread, muffins, etc. Most call for a brief resting in the pan after removal from the oven followed by a period of cooling out of the pan.
  Leaving bread or cake in the pan overly long after baking doesn't allow it to dry out; in addition to getting soggy, it may be difficult to remove from the pan as well.

- To check a roasting chicken or turkey, pierce the fleshy inside of the thigh with a sharp knife; the liquid will run clear if the bird is done.

Cutting, Slicing, and Serving:

❋ When cutting or slicing, always slide the blade and vary the pressure to suit the item being cut so that the knife does the work and not you. That goes for paring vegetables as well; slide the peeler back and forth to allow it to slice.
Forcing a blade through food tears it rather than cutting it.

❋ Allow roasted meat to rest for about fifteen minutes to permit the juices to set before slicing—carving will be easier and slices will be cut cleaner.

❋ Not enough serving platters for a buffet? Just cut a round, oval, rectangle, or whatever from the side of a corrugated carton and wrap in aluminum foil. Cover the foil with a layer of shredded lettuce and decorate with fluted fruit or cucumber slices before placing slices of meat or cheese, sandwiches, canapés, or unmolded salad (see next entry) on the platter. And you don't have to wash the tray!

❋ For an elegant presentation of tuna salad, potato salad, etc., lightly oil a serving bowl (or custard cup for an individual serving) and place thin strips or decorative slices of carrots, beets, pimientos, etc. in a pattern in the bottom. Carefully fill with the salad, pack it down well, and chill; just before serving, unmold the salad onto a serving platter or plate.

Equivalents and Substitutions:

❋ First, a quick review:

16 ounces by **weight** equals one pound
16 ounces by **volume** equals one pint
8 ounces by **volume** equals one cup
32 ounces by **volume** equals one quart

3 teaspoons (not 2) by **volume** equals one tablespoon
2 tablespoons by **volume** equals one ounce

Thus ¼ *cup* by volume equals *2 ounces* equals *4 tablespoons*. If you don't have a ¼ cup measure, 4 tablespoons will do, and it's often easier depending on what you are measuring. There are lots of other recipe measurements that can made easier if they are converted, but you'll have to do your own math.

Remember that **weight** and **volume** are not synonymous—the volume or space occupied by a pound of potato chips is much greater than that of a pound of beef. In addition, the density and moisture content of food directly influence its volume as compared to weight—the volume of that pound of potato chips will be reduced considerably if the chips are crushed and even more if they are soaked in water (yuck!).

We mentioned elsewhere that a recipe instruction to sift flour before measuring is an attempt to achieve uniformity—many chefs resolve this by measuring weight rather than volume when proportions are critical.

With all of this in mind, here are some approximations for relating weight and volume:

Almonds (with shells) 1 lb. = 4½ ounces shelled
(shelled) 1 lb. = 3 cups whole = 4 cups chopped
Apples (fresh) 1 lb. = 3 cups sliced or chopped
Bananas (fresh) 1 lb. = 2 cups sliced; 1½ cups mashed
Beans (fresh, green) 1 lb. = 3 cups
(dried) 1 lb. = 2 cups = 5½ cups cooked
Bread 1 slice soft = ½ cup soft crumbs
1 slice dry = $1/3$ cup dry crumbs
Butter 1 stick (¼ lb.) = 8 tablespoon = ½ cup
Cabbage (fresh) 1 lb. = 4 cups shredded = 2 cups cooked
Carrots (fresh) 1 lb. = 2½ to 3 cups shredded or sliced
Cheese (firm) 1 lb. = 4 cups grated
Coffee (ground) 1 lb. will make about 60 cups
Corn (fresh) 1 medium ear = ½ cup kernels
Corn meal 1 lb. = 3 cups dry = 4 cups cooked
Cream (heavy or whipping) 1 cup = 2 cups whipped
Eggplant (fresh) 1 lb. = 2 to 2½ cups diced
Eggs - see below
Flour (all-purpose wheat) 1 lb. = 3 cups sifted
(cake) 1 lb. = 4½ cups sifted
(whole wheat) 1 lb. = 3½ cups unsifted
Grits (quick) 1 lb. = 3 cups = 12 cups cooked
Hazelnuts (with shells) 1 lb. = 7 ounces shelled
(shelled) 1 lb. = 3½ cups
Lemons (medium) 2 tablespoons juice; 2 teaspoons zest
Mushrooms (fresh) 1 lb. = 5 cups sliced = 2 cups cooked
Oatmeal 1 lb. = 5 cups = 9 cups cooked
Onions (fresh) 1 lb. = about 2 cups sliced or chopped
Oranges (fresh) 1 lb. = about 1 cup juice

Pasta	1 lb. = 6 cups cooked
Pecans (with shells)	1 lb. = 6 ounces shelled
(shelled)	1 lb. = 4 cups
Rice (regular)	1 lb. = 2 cups = 6 cups cooked
Sugar (brown)	1 lb. = 2¼ cups packed
(confectioner's)	1 lb. = 4 cups unsifted
(granulated)	1 lb. = 2¼ cups
Tomatoes (fresh)	1 lb. = 1½ cups chopped
Walnuts (with shells)	1 lb. = 6 ounces shelled
(shelled)	1 lb. = 4 cups

⁕ When adjusting the size of a recipe, you often wind up needing to add part of an egg. To do so, mix an egg lightly, then measure: one tablespoon equals about a third of an egg; one and a half tablespoons, half of an egg.
It takes about five large eggs to make one cup.

Flavoring and Seasoning:

⁕ Sauces that are to be reduced should be seasoned after boiling down as the flavors are intensified during the reduction.

⁕ When substituting dried herbs for fresh, reduce the quantity by one-half to allow for their stronger flavor.

⁕ Improve the flavor of dried herbs by crushing them with a mortar and pestle or rubbing them in your hand before adding them to a recipe.

⁕ Buy dried herbs in quantities consistent with how often you use them; they lose much of their essence after about a year and should be replaced.

Miscellaneous Stuff:

⁕ When sautéing ingredients for a soup that is to be served cold, use oil in the pan, as butter will coagulate when chilled.

⁕ To get rid of odors on a cutting board, sprinkle the board with salt, allow to rest for a few minutes, then rub down with a lemon half.

⁕ To improve texture of a cream sauce, stir in a small amount of butter just before serving.

⁕ Chicken parts are expensive compared to the cost of a whole chicken... and cutting one up is not difficult. Instead of buying parts for a specific recipe, buy the whole chicken and plan a second meal around the remaining parts or accumulate them in the freezer for a future meal.

As a last resort, those odd chicken parts can be cooked and cut up to serve hot in a cream sauce or cold in a chicken salad.

- To prepare corn for adding to muffins or corn fritters, select fresh ears and slice through the center of each row of kernels; then use the back of the blade to scrape the meat from the cob.

- If the quantity and quality of protein in a meal is a matter of concern, there are foods, such as beans and rice, that combine to form complete proteins. Often only a small amount of meat, fish, egg, milk, butter, or cheese are necessary to supply the essential amino acids that may be lacking in a vegetable dish.

- To reduce fat intake, when browning or baking ground meat such as for hamburgers or meat loaf, pour off the fat as soon as it accumulates in the pan so that it is not reabsorbed into the meat.

- For more healthful meals, reduce the amount of meat served and increase the quantity and number of vegetable dishes. This is easier done in stews, casseroles, and one-dish meals where the meat won't be missed if there is enough to provide adequate flavoring and the dish is supplemented by the addition of savory beans.

- Use stale cookies for dessert toppings or pie crust.

- Use stale bread to make bread crumbs.

- To prevent food from sticking to a pan, allow it to heat before adding butter or oil.

- When oiling pans, use a paper towel or pastry brush to spread on just the right amount of oil or butter.

Mixing and Blending:

- To beat egg whites to optimum volume, allow the eggs to come to room temperature first.

- Heavy cream should be well-chilled, along with the bowl and beaters before whipping.

- When adding raw egg to a hot sauce, cool a little of the sauce and mix it into the egg first, then add the warmed egg mixture to the sauce off the fire to keep the egg from cooking before it is completely blended with the sauce. And don't allow the sauce to boil—it will curdle and separate.

* When adding sour cream to a heated sauce, cool the sauce first to prevent curdling. If the sauce is to be reheated, be sure not to allow it to boil for that too will cause it to curdle.

* When mixing ingredients in a bowl, place a damp towel under the bowl to keep it from sliding.

Seafood:

* Place thawed shrimp or fish in salted water for a few minutes before cooking to give it a fresh-caught smell and flavor.

* Most recipes suggest cooking fish until the meat flakes. Actually, it's better to stop cooking just before it flakes—the heat retained by the meat will finish the cooking and you'll be rewarded with moist, firm flesh.

Soup:

* Soup can be a quick and nutritious meal, but commercial varieties often have a high fat and sodium content—check the label and whenever possible, make your own. Same goes for those quick casseroles that call for cream-of-something soup; better to make your own sauce and eliminate the excess fat, sodium, and calories.

* If you don't create enough cuttings to maintain a stock pot, try accumulating those you do have: boil them up in a small amount of water, freeze them in a block (use a small food storage container), and save them in a freezer bag. You may want to keep separate bags for chicken, beef, and seafood. Then when enough has been collected, bring them out and make a stock for soup or sauce. Beef and chicken can be combined; but you probably will want to keep the fish stock separate.

* You don't have to have home-made stock to make soup. Wait until you have a collection of leftovers, then add whatever you need to fill out the ingredients.
Cut up beef or chicken from a previous meal to disguise them and combine beans or fresh vegetables with those on hand. Add a bit of bouillon or consommé if necessary, but do it after the soup has cooked for a bit—you'll be surprised at the

flavor that often results from a simple combination of meat and vegetables alone.

Storage and Resuscitation:

- ✸ Egg shells may seem solid, but they are porous. Refrigerate eggs in the carton to prevent odors from seeping into them and to retard spoilage.
- ✸ Peeled hard-boiled eggs keep well in the refrigerator if kept in water in a covered container.
- ✸ For best results when cooking eggs or adding them to a preparation, allow them to come to room temperature.
- ✸ Anything stored in the refrigerator or freezer should be well-wrapped or covered tightly to prevent the food from drying out and picking up (or contributing to) extraneous odors.
- ✸ Generally, food that has been defrosted should not be frozen again. That's because freezing does not kill bacteria, it only retards their growth; once the food is defrosted, those little suckers wake start over where they left off.

Vegetables:

- ✸ To get the most flavor from onions, celery, or carrots, sauté them lightly in butter before adding them to a preparation.
- ✸ Vegetables that are old but not yet spoiled may not look appetizing but age has often intensified their flavor. Dark mushrooms, limp carrots or celery, and even onions that chase you out of the kitchen when you cut into them have a lot to offer. Just throw them in a pot of water to make stock.